THE KRAYS
a screenplay

Philip Ridley was born in the East End of London, where he still lives and works. He studied painting at St Martin's School of Art and has exhibited widely throughout Europe. He has written three novels for adults and six novels for children, including: *Kindlekrax*, winner of the Smarties Prize for Children's Fiction and the W. H. Smith Mind-Boggling Books Award; and *Kasper in the Glitter*, shortlisted for the 1995 Whitbread Best Children's Novel Award. His highly acclaimed screenplay for *The Krays* (1990) – winner of the *Evening Standard* Best Film of the Year Award – was soon followed by his debut feature as both writer and director, *The Reflecting Skin* (1990), which won eleven international awards, was voted one of the Top Ten Films of the Year by the *Los Angeles Times* and prompted *Rolling Stone* magazine to describe him as 'a visionary'. In 1991 he was awarded the Most Promising Newcomer to British Film at the *Evening Standard* Film Awards. His second feature film *The Passion of Darkly Noon* (1995), a cult classic, won the Best Director Prize at the Fantasporto International Film Festival. His first stage play, the award-winning *The Pitchfork Disney*, was premiered at the Bush Theatre, London, in 1991. His second stage play, *The Fastest Clock in the Universe*, was premiered at the Hampstead Theatre, London, in 1992 and won the Meyer-Whitworth Prize, a *Time Out* Award, and both the Critics' Circle and the *Evening Standard* Award for Most Promising Playwright – the only time the *Evening Standard* has given the Most Promising Award to the same person twice, for both film and theatre. *Ghost from a Perfect Place*, his third stage play, was premiered at the Hampstead Theatre in 1994. His work has been translated into sixteen languages, including Japanese.

THE KRAYS

a screenplay by
Philip Ridley

Methuen Film

A METHUEN SCREENPLAY

Published by Methuen

The Krays screenplay copyright © 1997 by Philip Ridley
Introduction copyright © 1997 by Philip Ridley
Philip Ridley has asserted his right under the Copyright, Designs and Patents Act,
1988 to be identified as the author of this work.
'The Rogue In Vogue' lyrics © 1997 by Philip Ridley
Photographs © 1997 by Richard Blanshard

First published in the United Kingdom in 1997 by Methuen,
Random House, 20 Vauxhall Bridge Road, London SW1V 2SA

Random House Australia (Pty) Limited
20 Alfred Street, Milsons Point, Sydney,
New South Wales 2061, Australia

Random House New Zealand Limited
18 Poland Road, Glenfield
Auckland 10, New Zealand

Random House South Africa (Pty) Limited
Endulini, 5A Jubilee Road, Parktown 2193, South Africa

Random House UK Limited Reg. No. 954009

A CIP catalogue record for this book
is available from the British Library

ISBN 0 413 711307

Typeset in 10 on 13.5 point Plantin Light
by Wilmaset Ltd, Birkenhead, Wirral
Printed and bound in Great Britain
by Cox & Wyman Ltd, Reading, Berkshire

for Peter Medak –
who filmed the dream

AUTHOR'S NOTE

FROM A RADIO INTERVIEW WITH PHILIP RIDLEY
LONDON FILM FESTIVAL 1996

You were born in the East End of London during the sixties. Do you remember stories of the Krays from your childhood?

Very much so. I was born in Bethnal Green, the same area as the Krays. Vallance Road, where they lived, was just a few streets away. Of course, I was very young at the time. But I've got vivid memories of people clustered together, gossiping about violence and murder. I remember one particular night, laying in bed and listening to my Mum, Grandmother and Aunts discuss how the Krays had beaten someone unconscious. Then ran over his body in their car. 'They deliberately aimed for his head,' I remember someone saying. 'They crushed it!' This image of a crushed head haunted me for ages. I couldn't look at a head without imagining it flat as a pancake.

It's interesting you remember the women, not the men, talking about violence.

Well, the sixties was a time of relatively full employment in East London. So I grew up in a predominantly female environment.

You say in one of your novels, 'I lived my childhood on the street of women, where men were invisible.'

During the day, men *were*. They were out at work. Men came home at night. This was the only period children spent with their Dads. I remember my Dad hurt himself at work once – he crushed a finger or something (he worked with woodworking machinery) – and he had to have some time off work. It was the weirdest feeling. I could barely think of what to say to him during the day. It was only at night – when the ritual was restored – that Dad and I could get on as normal.

And the story about the crushed head? Was it true?

Who knows? There are so many stories about the Krays in East London. Everyone seems to have one.

Have you?

Afraid so, yes. It happened when I was three or four years old. I was out shopping with my Grandmother down Bethnal Green Road market. It was near Easter and, as we walked past a stall, I caught sight of a particularly large chocolate egg. It was wrapped in golden foil. I said I wanted it. Gran said I couldn't have it. It was too expensive. I started crying. Still Gran refused. I screamed and screamed. And then . . . a man stepped forward. He was wearing a black suit and tie. Everyone round the stall went very quiet. The man in the black suit kissed me on the forehead, took a five pound note from his pocket and said to my Gran, 'Give the kid what he wants!' So I got my golden egg. And the man who bought it – the man in the black suit – was Ronnie Kray.

That actually happened? You remember it?

Put it this way: I've been told the story so much that – yes – I *do* remember it. As to whether it's one hundred per cent factual – who knows? As I said, everyone from East London has a Kray story. They can't all have really happened. But that doesn't stop them having a kind of truth. In a way, they explain things – a kind of emotional truth, if you like – far more eloquently than the facts.

'Unreal but true' is a good way of describing your screenplay.

I hope so, yes.

You never contemplated a drama-documentary approach, then?

To be honest, it's not really a case of 'contemplated' or 'not contemplated'. It's just not what I do. I pick up a pen and start writing. I'm not conscious of a style.

But your work does *have a very distinctive style.*

What I'm saying is, I'm not *conscious* of that style. Not while I'm working. I don't contrive it. It just happens. You know, while I was a teenager, I studied drawing with the artist Cecil Collins and he kept telling me, 'You create in order to understand, you don't understand in order to create. That's the way it works.' And, in a way, that's what I mean about style. Style is something that happens after the event.

You were still studying painting at St Martin's School of Art when you started writing The Krays, *weren't you?*

Yes.

So is it fair to say you approached it with a painter's sensibility?

Well . . . there are three answers to that question: yes, no, maybe. And I'm not saying that to be deliberately awkward. I really don't know. A lot of people think that because my filmmaking is full of images, then it must be because I studied painting. But this implies a very limited view of painting – painting as a figurative form of expression. But, you know, when I was at St Martin's, hardly anyone was expressing themselves figuratively. Most people were into pickling goldfish or pushing knitting-needles through their genitals.

But your work was figurative.

That's right. But there's a big – huge! – difference between the way I approach images in my paintings, and images in film. The essence of a film image is that – for the most part – it moves. It's why still images from a film are almost always disappointing. Also, most film images are about *sound* as well as image. And film images are not meant to be seen in isolation. Each image in a film is also about the image *before* it and the image *after* it. Paintings, for the most part, are isolated, soundless and static. The only thing I can say with any certainty is that some subject matter crosses over from my painting into my film work. And the fact that I tend to see the colours and composition of every shot. For example, the two colours that run through *The Krays* are black and white. The white of the swan, the black of the twins' suits, the white of Frances' wedding dress, the black of the Krays' hair.

Sounds like a painter talking to me.

Well, it sounds like a filmmaker to me. Film *is* a visual medium after all. An attempt to tell a story through images. Oh, I don't know . . . perhaps I'm just hyper-touchy about being labelled a painter-turned-filmmaker. You know, all style and no content.

When did your interest in film start?

It's always been there. I took lots of photographs when I was a child, then I had a Super 8 camera, then video. In fact, I did just as much film work at St Martin's as I did painting.

So how did you go from student films to The Krays?

A combination of things really. I'd published a couple of short stories, *Embracing Verdi* and *Leviathan*. They'd received quite a lot of attention. Also, word was out that I'd just signed a deal with Penguin for my novel, *In the Eyes of Mr Fury*. But, I suppose, the most important thing was the luck of being in the right place at the right time: I was working as a storyboard artist for a film company in the West End of London. This company was making a pop video for Spandau Ballet. And Gary and Martin Kemp – members of the band – wanted to make a film about the Krays. So, with my reputation as an East End writer . . . as I say, right place, right time.

Your screenplay hardly takes the conventional approach. It must have surprised them.

Some aspects of it were quite contentious at first, yes.

Such as?

The main thing was what we talked about earlier: this unreal but true approach. In other words, ignoring the facts.

Trying to, hopefully, create some kind of mythical, emotional truth.

And you did no research at all?

Well, I knew the basic facts: The twins were born in the East End of London, they were close to their mother, Ronnie was gay, Reggie was straight, Reggie married Frances, Frances committed suicide, the twins murdered two people, Jack the Hat and Joseph Cornell. The only research I did beyond that was talk to people in East London. I asked them what they remembered about that period. And, although I never used any of these anecdotes in the screenplay, they helped create an atmosphere of folklore.

There's definitely a feeling of modern myth about the film. Is that why you used the image of the swan?

You know, the swan was always there. Right from the very beginning. And Violet's voice-over saying, 'Shall I tell you my dream?' I always knew that's how I wanted the film to begin. It was a way of putting all my cards on the table from the start. A way of saying, 'This is not going to be what you expect'. That whole opening sequence works like an operatic overture: all the film's themes are there – dreams, myth, family, violence, blood.

What other aspects of the screenplay surprised people?

The fact that I wanted to concentrate on the women. Especially the mother, Violet. In many ways this was the most controversial thing. Everyone assumed that the mother would play an important part in any film about the Krays, but probably not to the lengths I wanted to push it. And certainly not including all the other women so much as well:

the Grandmother, the Aunts, Frances, the wives, the girlfriends. But, for me, this was the main fascination. I wanted to root the story in the domestic: discussions about bone-china cutlery, dog's mess being trod up the stairs, Violet bringing a tray of tea and biscuits into a gang meeting. This domestic environment – this brood of unconditionally loving women, is what the film is really about as far as I'm concerned. The right way to love, the wrong way to love: this is the film's subject. Everything else is camouflage.

At one point Violet says something like, 'I don't think you can love too much, but you can love in the wrong way.'

Exactly, and the twins carry on this wrong kind of loving in their own lives. Reggie with Frances. And Ronnie with his gay partner.

Did your approach to Ron's sexuality surprise people?

Of course. But . . . well, I wanted to treat Ron's homosexual affair as matter-of-fact and everyday as Reg's heterosexual one. I didn't want to make anything special of it.

Was there any resistance to that?

Very much so. Many financiers and distributors felt that we should have a scene where Ron's sexual orientation was discussed. You know the kind of thing: reaction shots of macho gang members looking shocked and going 'Ugh!' Or a scene where someone says, 'Ron's an all right bloke, even though he's a poof'. Or – even worse! – they didn't want Ron gay at all. They'd tell me, 'There's no *point* to him being gay. It doesn't affect the story.'

How did you reply to that?

I said, 'There's no *point* to the twins having black hair, but that doesn't mean they should be blond.'

So you wouldn't change it?

No way.

What about the film's general homo-erotic tone?

Well, to be honest, most financiers wouldn't recognise homo-eroticism if it looked like Brad Pitt, wore Calvin Kleins and said, 'Fancy a rim job, Big Boy.'

Talking of Big Boys . . . your screenplay concentrates on the opposite: Little Boys. The childhood of the twins. Presumably this was another surprise.

Yes. But childhood has always been a big theme in my work. The two short stories and novel I mentioned earlier, all of them were through the eyes of a child. So it seemed obvious to me to open with Ronnie and Reggie as children. It was the most enjoyable section to write. Every scene is made up: sheltering from bombs in Bethnal Green tube station, fights in the school playground, Aunt Rose buying toy crocodiles, the twins dreaming about flying, their Grandfather telling them stories about Jack the Ripper. It was like writing an original story. Total fiction.

So how did financiers react to the screenplay as a whole?

Like the crew of the Nostromo seeing the chest-burster for the first time.

They didn't appreciate your approach?

Hated it. Apart from all the things we've just discussed, their main concern was lack of sympathetic characters. They'd say, 'The problem is . . . the audience won't care for Ron and Reg.' And I'd say, 'It doesn't matter – they'll be fascinated.' And they'd say, 'But it's a screenplay without a hero.' And I'd say, 'The swan is the hero.' And they'd say, 'Get out of my office, you arty wanker.' It went on like that for quite a time. A really depressing time.

And, I guess, being a story everyone knew – or thought they knew – everyone had an opinion on how the story should be done.

Well, of course. All I heard was: 'You should have done this', 'You should have done that', 'You missed the part out where Ronnie did this . . .', 'You missed the part where Reggie did that . . .'

How did you react?

I took lots of paracetamol and codeine, ate chocolate and recited the mantra: 'Opinions are like arseholes, everyone's got one.'

But, eventually, it did get financed.

I've always believed it was the actors that kept the project going. Not just Gary and Martin, although, of course, they were instrumental. But the fact that, while nearly every financier in the country was turning the project down, more and more actors read the script and wanted to be part of it: Billie Whitelaw, Steven Berkoff, Tom Bell, Susan Fleetwood, Charlotte Cornwell, Kate Hardy – a cast to die for. So that, in the end, something had to give. But to be honest, I don't know much about the final stages of putting the film together because, by that time, I was in America working on *The Reflecting Skin*.

Your first film as director?

That's right.

Is that why you didn't direct The Krays?

Oh, no. The possibility of me directing *The Krays* was never discussed. It was always a project written for someone else. In this case, Peter Medak.

In many ways, Medak was a strange choice: a mid-European emigree, who worked briefly in London during the sixties, and now lives in Hollywood.

It's that very strangeness that made him so right. As you say, Peter worked in London during the period the Krays were at their zenith. But Peter, coming from abroad, was already seeing these events as an outsider. Then he went to Hollywood to work. This meant, when approaching *The Krays* script, he did so in exactly the same spirit in which it was written: as a time recalled. Peter filmed how he *remembered* that period. It's this aspect that helps give the film such a chilling, cold atmosphere, I think. The audience, hopefully, watches the film like they would a snake in a glass tank. Repelled and fascinated in equal measure.

Did the censors want any cuts?

The violence was always a problem for them. It's strange when you consider how violent films went soon after the release of *The Krays*. But, of course, that's violence coming from America: violence being used as excitement. Cartoon-violence. But *The Krays* . . . Oh, *The Krays* was different. It was a home-grown product. And the violence was repulsive and disgusting.

Surely that was the point?

I always thought so. You know, I worked very hard to make the violence have some kind of emotional impact. That's why – when people get hurt – it's usually on their face, or – in one instance – their palm. Maximum wince factor.

The most notorious scene, I suppose, is the sword through the mouth.

Well, to be precise, it's a sabre. But everyone refers to it as the sword in the mouth scene. And that's the scene the censors wanted cut. In fact, we *did* lose a shot from that. But it was something Medak always had a feeling we'd lose. That's why he shot it. I remember him saying to me, 'To make this scene work properly, it's got to be really horrific. If we do it that way, we might lose the whole thing. So I'll give the censors an extra gratuitous shot – cutting this will be our token gesture to appease them.' And that's exactly what happened. The politics of art, eh?

What was the shot?

In the scene as you see it, the violence is shot from behind the victim's head. But the scene was also shot from *in front* – so you actually *see* the victim's face. It's that image that ended up on the cutting-room floor.

But nothing else was lost?

Not in the sense of being *forced* to lose it, no. But certain things were edited or trimmed. And there were several scenes that were never filmed due to lack of time. A few moments with the Frances character were cut. But this was mainly because Kate Hardy is such an emotionally true actor. She has the ability to skin herself alive on film in the way few English actors can. As such, some of my work became redundant . . . but there is one whole scene with Frances I do regret losing. It happens when the whole Kray clan go to the nightclub for the evening. Shortly before Frances' suicide. The twins are notorious by now and, like any celebrities, surrounded by photographers. Everyone enjoys the attention except Frances. She jumps at every camera flash. Unable to take it, she goes to the bathroom. It's this bathroom scene that's missing.

What happens?

Well, it's a scene between Frances and Iris. Frances talks about her inability to cope. She asks Iris for advice, for help. But Iris basically tells her to turn a blind eye and get on with it. The scene was important to me for lots of reasons, but two in particular. Firstly, it showed that – in their own way – the women were every bit as ruthless as the men. If anyone got in their way, they'd walk right over them. And that included a female family-member on the brink of a breakdown. And, secondly, it was a way of re-emphasising that the women – and, by implication, this includes Violet – knew exactly what the twins were up to.

But, surely, even without this scene, it's still perfectly clear that all the women – and Violet most of all – knew.

I would have thought so, yes. But some people find it ambiguous. Don't get me wrong – I'm not against ambiguity. Usually, I'm for all the ambiguity I can get. But, in this case, I think that – in the end – you *have* to decide that Violet knows. It's what the film is about. Her knowing, but not acknowledging. That's the drama. That's the tragedy.

The thing that surprised me the most was the absence of police.

That surprised a lot of people. 'Where's the police? We've got to have the police.' But that wasn't the story I was interested in telling. For me, the police were irrelevant. Worse, they were uncinematic. English police *must* be the most uncinematic police force in the world. That goes for their cars too.

But I'm sure it's what most financiers wanted.

Of course it was. Diligent detectives tracking down their men. Handcuffs. Sirens. The chase is on. 'Alright, Mr Kray, you're nicked!' The financiers wanted this because they saw it as the voice of morality. There'd be scenes with coppers saying, 'They're a nasty lot, these Krays. They hurt people. And they're going to pay. Society will be avenged.' And the audience would heave a collective sigh of relief. They'd feel comfortable.

But you didn't want them to feel comfortable.

Not in that sense, no.

And you didn't want a moral?

Certainly not.

Several critics condemned this immorality.

Well, it might not be moral. But it's definitely not *im*moral.

Then what is it?

Hopefully, it's *a*moral.

Why hopefully?

Well, it's not an artist's job to take a moral standpoint. It's just their job to tell their characters' story. There's no yardstick for morality, anyway. There are no absolutes. And, in art, what you end up with is either the prevailing morality of the day (and nothing dates quicker than morality), or you get a legal morality – what the law will *allow* you to show. And this means focusing on certain images or acts. So . . . seeing an erect penis is considered immoral. But who says? Who makes these decisions? Heterosexual, homophobic males who can't get a hard-on presumably. The only immoral thing about *The Krays* was that, at the first press screening, half the critics turned up late, talked through the whole film, and left before the end. The reason there were so few sarcastic comments about the flying swan was that most critics didn't see it.

But if these critics genuinely didn't like the concept of the film, they might consider their behaviour totally moral.

That proves my point. No absolutes. One person's moral statement is another person's ignorant critic.

Most critics, though, were enthusiastic for the film. And it was a big commercial success. Did that surprise you?

The scale of it did, yes. Especially in America. They loved the film there.

And its reputation continues to grow.

I'm glad to say it does.

Why, do you think?

Well, I'd like to think it's because of the flying swan, the childhood, the strong women, the crocodiles, the homo-eroticism . . . but it's probably because someone gets a sword in the mouth.

THE KRAYS

PETER: (*Passionately*) I don't want to go to school and learn solemn things. No-one is going to catch me, Lady, and make me a man. I want always to be a little boy and have fun.

(from *Peter Pan* by J. M. Barrie)

CAST

RONNIE KRAY	Gary Kemp
REGGIE KRAY	Martin Kemp
VIOLET KRAY	Billie Whitelaw
ROSE	Susan Fleetwood
MAY	Charlotte Cornwell
HELEN	Avis Bunnage
CANNONBALL LEE	Jimmy Jewel
FRANCES	Kate Hardie
CHARLIE SENIOR	Alfred Lynch
CHARLIE JUNIOR	Roger Monk
IRIS	Pattie Love
JACK THE HAT	Tom Bell
CORNELL	Steven Berkoff
STEVE	Gary Love
MRS LAWSON	Barbara Ferris
MR LAWSON	Victor Spinetti
EDDIE PELLAM	Philip Bloomfield
SHOPKEEPER	Norman Rossington
REFEREE	Michael Balfour
PERRY	Jimmy Flint
DENNIS	Andrew Kitchen
EDDIE	Michael Carr
WHIP	Ian Burfield
GREY	Bob Brimson
TERRY	Russell Gold
DICKIE	David Arlen
SAM RIPLEY	Jon McKenna
CHRIS RIPLEY	Sean Blower
NEWSAGENT	Murray Melvin
SHARON	Sadie Frost
POLICEMAN	Stephen Lewis
REGAL MANAGER	Pete Turner
JACK'S GIRLFRIEND	Soo Dronet
BOXER	John H. Stracey
YOUNG DOCTOR	David Fenwick
IVY	Laura Cox
PALENDRI	Angus MacInnes
ITALIAN GANGSTER	Michael Tezcan
MAN CUT OUTSIDE REGAL	Richard Vanstone
YOUNG EDDIE	Chris Pitt
MARK	Mark Burdis
MAN IN FIGHT	Pete Gillett

2

MIDWIFE	Julie May
ANGRY CUSTOMER	Jackie Downey
TEACHER	Vernon Dobtchett
STEVE'S FRIEND	Ryan Ward
BARMAID	Chrissie Coterill
LOST BOY	Simon Foy
LOST BOY	Tony Sands
MALTESE GANGSTER	Behrouz Behnejad
BOY IN CLASSROOM	Matthew Barnet
CHARLIE AGED 12	Benjamin Brazier
RON AGED 1	John Paul White
REG AGED 1	Michael White
RON AGED 3	Harlon Haveland
REG AGED 3	Sam Haveland
RON AGED 12	Jason Bennett
REG AGED 12	Jamie Bennett
STRAKER	Jimmy Balten
FRANK	Brian Nichels
BILL	Dave Courtney
TOM	Ben Mansworth
Director	Peter Medak
Writer	Philip Ridley
Producers	Dominic Anciano
	Ray Burdis
Director of Photography	Alex Thomson BSc
Music	Michael Kamen
Editor	Martin Walsh
Production Designer	Michael Pickwood
Costume Designer	Lindy Hemming

BLACK SCREEN

VIOLET (*voice over, East London accent, magically cooing*):
    Shall I tell you my dream?
    Cut to . . .

EXT. SWAN IN FLIGHT. DAY
A grainy, black and white image of a beautiful swan in flight.
Slow motion. The sound of the wings amplified.

VIOLET (*voice over*): . . . I dreamt I was . . . a beautiful
    white swan . . . and I could fly anywhere . . . do
    anything . . . I ate fish and pecked at things with my
    beak . . .

INT. KRAY HOUSE, VIOLET'S BEDROOM. NIGHT
VIOLET's *face in close-up. She is about thirty, screaming, face*
covered in sweat, in great agony. We don't know where we are
or why she is screaming. This, too, is in black and white.

EXT. SWAN IN FLIGHT. DAY
The swan continues flying . . .

VIOLET (*voice over*): And I had this egg . . . a beautiful egg
    it was . . . And there were noises coming from inside the
    shell . . .

5

INT. KRAY HOUSE, VIOLET'S BEDROOM. NIGHT

VIOLET's *hand clutches at the sheets. She is still screaming, back arching, convulsing.*

We become aware of shadows moving round her – other people . . . a MIDWIFE, *holding a basin of hot water, trying to force her way between* ROSE *and* MAY, VIOLET's *sisters.*

ROSE *is strikingly beautiful, also about thirty.* MAY, *a little older, lacks* ROSE's *looks but has a strong, determined face. Of the two, it's her you'd rely on in a crisis.*

Also in the room is HELEN, VIOLET's *mother.* HELEN *is the strongest looking of the women. A strength that comes from having seen it all before. She is sometimes thought of as heartless, but is, in reality, merely pragmatic.*

VIOLET (*voice over*): And do you know what the noises were
    . . . They – now listen carefully – they were children's
    voices . . .

EXT. SWAN IN FLIGHT. DAY

The swan flies closer. The sounds of its wings gets louder . . .

VIOLET (*voice over*): And I looked after this egg . . . I kept it
    warm and safe. Until, one day, there was a hatching
    sound . . .

INT. KRAY HOUSE, VIOLET'S BEDROOM. NIGHT

VIOLET *is obviously in the throes of childbirth: shrieking, gleaming with sweat, face a rictus of pain.*

VIOLET: Oh, my God! Mum!

    MIDWIFE, ROSE, MAY *and* HELEN *are encouraging*
    VIOLET.

HELEN (*urgently*): Push, Vi! Push!

    VIOLET's *screams are getting louder and louder.*

ROSE: Push, Violet! Come on!

MAY: You can do it!

> VIOLET *is clawing at the sheets.* ROSE *wipes sweat from* VIOLET*'s face.*

VIOLET (*screaming*): Mum! Mum! Mum!

> *Suddenly, blood crawls over the bedsheets. And – with the blood – we lose the black and white. We see the red of the blood.*
>
> > *The rest of the film will be in colour.*
> >
> > ROSE *stands, looks . . .*

ROSE: It's twins, Vi.

INT. CHURCH, 1934. DAY

VIOLET *is standing at the font. She is holding the twins. We see other people's hands in shot, but not their faces.*

> *A* PRIEST *is baptising the children.*

PRIEST: . . . Renounce the devil and all his works . . . I christen you Ronald Kray . . . I christen you Reginald Kray . . . in the name of the Father, the Son and the Holy Ghost –

EXT. KRAY HOUSE, 1936. DAY

A street of red brick, two storey terraced houses. The sun is shining, the sound of laughter. Colours are vivid. A yearning memory of perfect childhood.

> *A* POSTMAN *walks down the street, sorting through some letters.*

VIOLET *is on her knees cleaning her doorstep. She is wearing an apron, hard at work, enjoying every minute of it.*

> *The* TWINS *are nearby, playing on the pavement. They are dressed identically: beautiful and menacing in equal measure. Their hair a little too black, eyes too blue, skin too flawless: terrifying perfection.*

7

POSTMAN *passes by* VIOLET.

VIOLET: Morning, Frank. Anything for us?

POSTMAN: Not today, Mrs Kray.

> VIOLET *looks across the street. A* NEIGHBOUR *has just come out of her house with a bucket. She gets down on her knees and starts cleaning her doorstep.* VIOLET *shoots her a look: About time too, it says. The* NEIGHBOUR *glares back as defiantly as possible, but a single glance from* VIOLET *could crack a lobster at twenty paces.*

> *The* TWINS *chuckle as they play.* VIOLET *directs her attention to them, smiling proudly.*

VIOLET: Who loves you, eh? Who loves you little monsters.

RON and REG (*gleefully*): Mum . . .

VIOLET: That's right, Mummy loves you. Mummy loves you more than anything. More than all the cakes, all the jewellery and all the chocolate in the world . . . That's how much your Mummy loves you.

> ROSE *comes out of her house next door. She smiles at the* TWINS.

ROSE: Hello, boys.

> *Then* ROSE *sees* NEIGHBOUR *opposite, cleaning her doorstep.*

ROSE (*indicating* NEIGHBOUR): Vi! Vi!

VIOLET: I know. I've seen. Miracles never cease.

> MAY *comes rushing out of her house now. She has seen the* NEIGHBOUR *cleaning her doorstep too. This is obviously big news on the street.*

MAY: Vi! Rose!

VIOLET and ROSE: We know.

MAY: It's about time, I say.

ROSE: She's let herself go.

> *Now* HELEN *is rushing up. She's obviously seen the* NEIGHBOUR *cleaning her doorstep too.*

HELEN: Vi. . . ! Rose! May! She's . . .

VIOLET, ROSE and MAY (*together*): Cleaning her doorstep!

HELEN *joins them, breathless with excitement.*

HELEN: Dirty cow. I told her, you know. She had toast between her teeth. Made me feel sick.

The TWINS *playing is getting almost hysterical now.*

VIOLET (*going over to them*): Come on, boys . . . Mummy's trying to talk.

One of the TWINS *hits out at* VIOLET.

It's only a slap – and VIOLET *could hardly have felt it – but she reacts as if really hurt.*

VIOLET: Oh . . . what have you done? Hurt Mummy! Hurt Mummy!

VIOLET *feigns tears, buries her face in her hands.* HELEN, ROSE *and* MAY *come over to comfort* VIOLET.

HELEN (*to the* TWINS): What have you done, you naughty boys?

MAY: Hurt Mummy.

ROSE: Poor Mummy. All hurt.

It's only a game of course, and the women are having a great time, barely able to conceal their laughter through mock tears and outrage.

But, for the TWINS, *it's horrifying.*

They've hurt their Mummy: their world is collapsing.

They toddle over to VIOLET *and wrap their arms around her. The* TWINS *are almost hysterical with tears.*

TWINS: Sorry . . . Mummy . . . sorry.

VIOLET: You must never hurt Mummy.

TWINS: Never hurt Mummy.

INT. KRAY HOUSE, VIOLET'S BEDROOM, 1941. NIGHT

It is late at night. Moonlight through curtains.

Both VIOLET *and* CHARLIE SENIOR *in deep sleep.*

CHARLIE SENIOR *is snoring.*

Suddenly there is a cough from the next room. It's barely audible, but VIOLET*'s eyes click open at once. One of her children is ill, and the maternal radar is beeping alarm.*

She gets out of bed automatically. Starts struggling into her dressing gown. She glances down at CHARLIE SENIOR. *He is still snoring, oblivious to it all.* VIOLET *leaves the bedroom and rushes down –*

INT. KRAY HOUSE, UPPER HALLWAY. NIGHT
– wrapping dressing gown around her.

VIOLET (*under her breath*): Ron . . .
    She opens the TWINS´ *bedroom door and –*

INT. KRAY HOUSE, TWINS' BEDROOM. NIGHT
– rushes in. The TWINS *are in bed. They are older now, about five or six.* RON *is coughing, flushed and sweating.* REG *is awake, staring at* RON; *half worried, half fascinated.*

REG (*pointing at* RON): Mum! Look! Mum!
VIOLET: It's alright, darling. Mummy's here!
    VIOLET *dashes straight to* RON *and feels his forehead.*
VIOLET (*intensely concerned*): What's wrong with you,
    darling? Can you hear me? It's Mummy, darling.
    Mummy . . .

INT. HOSPITAL WARD. DAY
The ward is harsh, impersonal, more like a prison than a place of care – and we get the feeling the patients are treated with similar severity.
    It's visiting time: general bustle.
    Nurses rushing.
    Tea trolley.

Relatives, weeping and confused.

RON *is in one of the beds, he is still feverish, floating in and out of delirium.* VIOLET *sits on the bed, holding* RON's *hand. She is studying him with an instinct, more potent than any dispassionate medic. A primaeval understanding of her own flesh and blood.*

ROSE, MAY *and* HELEN *stand like sentinels around the bed.*

A DOCTOR *hovers nearby. He is young – early twenties and obviously daunted by the sheer physical presence of the Kray women. And so he should be; in their present mood (protecting one of their young) they'd intimidate an army.*

VIOLET: He hasn't got enough blankets. It's freezing in
    here. He'll leave here in a wooden overcoat if you
    don't –

DOCTOR: Mrs Kray, I –

VIOLET: What do you think, Mum?

HELEN: Goosebumps. All over.

DOCTOR: It's diptheria, Mrs Kray . . .

VIOLET: I could have told you that. Days ago. Arctic
    conditions a cure now are they?

DOCTOR: In the circumstances –

ROSE: How old are you?

DOCTOR: Sorry?

ROSE: How old?

DOCTOR: Twenty-four. Nearly.

ROSE: What? Twenty-three and three quarters or something
    . . . Look, Vi, this is bloody ridiculous.

DOCTOR: Mrs Kray, I –

VIOLET: May, get me his coat. I'm taking him home.

DOCTOR: B . . . but you can't!

    VIOLET *glares at him.* ROSE *and* MAY *and* HELEN *do
    the same.*

    The DOCTOR *is visibly petrified. His blood already
    solidifying, turning to stone.*

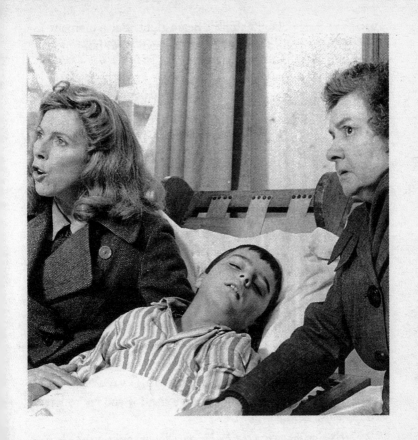

VIOLET: Sorry? Don't think I heard right. For a moment I
    thought you said I can't take me own child home –
DOCTOR (*faintly*): It's against the rules.
VIOLET: Not *my* rules. There's only *one* rule here. And
    that's keeping my son alive. I brought him here and
    you've done bugger all . . .
    As VIOLET *speaks,* ROSE *pushes past the doctor and takes*
    RONNIE *from the bed.* ROSE, HELEN *and* MAY *start to*
    dress the child.
        The DOCTOR *is helpless. He looks pathetically round*
    for support.
        The rest of the ward has noticed the commotion.
    Relatives, patients and nurses are staring. But the Kray
    women are a daunting quartet – nobody rushes to the
    DOCTOR*'s aid!*
VIOLET: I know what's best for him. What do you know?
    See straight through you. Like one of your bloody
    x-rays.
DOCTOR: But . . .
    ROSE *gives the fully dressed* RONNIE *to* VIOLET.
VIOLET: I'm taking him out of here. And if you try to stop
    me . . . Rose!
    ROSE *grabs* DOCTOR *by his shirt collar, pulls it so tight he*
    almost gags, then brings her other hand – now a clenched
    fist – up to his chin.
ROSE: Don't tempt me, there's a good boy. Because I will,
    you know. God help me. I will.
HELEN: Men! They know nothing! They never have done
    and never will.
    VIOLET, ROSE, MAY *and* HELEN *start leaving the ward,*
    holding RON *lovingly between them –*
VIOLET: I know what Ron needs and it's not here.
ROSE: He needs Reg.

VIOLET: You're right, Rose. He needs Reg. They don't
know what he wants. All they got is words. Well, I've
got words too . . .

VIOLET *turns back to face the ward. Everyone – doctors,
nurses and patients – is staring.*

VIOLET: Bollocks to the lot of you!

EXT. KRAY HOUSE, 1942. DAY

*The Second World War has taken its toll on the street.
Several houses have been bombed. Piles of rubble everywhere.
Some people sit in armchairs and sofas they've managed to
salvage from their wrecked homes.*

INT. KRAY HOUSE, LIVING ROOM. DAY

CHARLIE SENIOR – *the* TWINS' *Dad – is asleep in an
armchair. He is middle-aged, tired, a vague ghost of a man.*
VIOLET *is tidying the room around him.*

RON *and* REG – *now about eight-years-old – are tickling
their sleeping father's nose. It's like a game to them. The*
TWINS *are dressed identically. They are very smart and clean:
two little demonic angels.*

VIOLET: Reggie, take your fingers out of Dad's nose. I've
told you before. There's germs up there.

REGGIE: Ow, Mum.

VIOLET: Don't 'Ow, Mum' me. There's a million and one
places to put your fingers without putting them up your
Dad's nose.

RON: But he's asleep.

VIOLET: Good! Don't wake him. I don't want him under my
feet as well.

VIOLET *looks around the room. She notices the mirror
above the mantelpiece is slightly crooked. She tuts and goes
to straighten it.*

15

REG: Like fairy-story.

VIOLET: What's that?

RON: Dad. Like Snow White. Asleep after he ate the apple from the witch –

REG: – The half with poison.

VIOLET: I should be so lucky.

RON *goes to kiss his Dad.*

VIOLET: What you doing now?

RON: Kissing Dad –

REG: – See if he wakes up.

VIOLET: Don't be disgusting. No-one kisses your Dad.

The TWINS *stare at* VIOLET. *She looks back at them, lovingly.*

VIOLET: Look. Why don't you go and see your Aunt Rose. She's got something for you, you know.

RON and REG: What?

VIOLET: Go and find out!

The TWINS *rush out, giggling with excitement.*

VIOLET (*calling*): And don't make a nuisance of yourselves!

VIOLET *turns and stares into the mirror. She studies her reflection for a while.*

VIOLET (*softly sighing*): Mirror, mirror on the wall . . .

EXT. KRAY HOUSE. DAY

RON *and* REG *rush out of their house and go next door to –*

INT. ROSE'S HOUSE, LIVING ROOM. DAY

– where ROSE *is dusting a wooden table in the middle of the room.*

RON: Aunt Rose!

REG: Aunt Rose!

RON: Mum said –

REG: – You got something –

RON: – For us!

ROSE (*chuckling*): Calm down, you two.

> RON *and* REG *sit at the table.* ROSE *gets two brown paper bags, then sits at the table with them.*
>
> ROSE *gives a bag to* RON *and* REG. *They each remove a wooden crocodile from the bags.*

REG: What are they?

RON: I know! Monsters!

ROSE: Not monsters . . . crocodiles!

> *The* TWINS *start to play with their wooden toys.*

ROSE: They come from the jungle. Some are really big. As big as this room. Everything is afraid of them. And when they're dead . . . they make shoes and handbags out of them. Expensive things they are.

REG: What do they eat?

ROSE: Men. (*Notices scratches on surface of table.*) Oh, where do all these scratches come from?

RON: Is there lots of blood?

ROSE: Lots.

> ROSE *starts polishing the table . . .*

INT. KRAY HOUSE, PARLOUR/BACK YARD. DAY

VIOLET *is sitting at table, peeling potatoes.* HELEN *sits opposite, pouring tea.* AUNT MAY *sits on armchair, reading newspaper.*

Through a window into back yard, we can see CANNON-BALL LEE, *the* TWINS' *grandfather. He is teaching* CHARLIE JUNIOR, *the* TWINS' *brother, how to box.*

VIOLET: I just hope Rose doesn't spoil them. That's all. God knows, she hasn't got two brass farthings to rub together, yet every time they go there she gives them something. No wonder they're there so much.

Sometimes think I'm only here to cook their meals and wash their clothes.

HELEN: She means well, Vi.

VIOLET: I know she means well, Mum. But that's not the point. It's all this love pouring out.

MAY: But the twins are so lovely, Vi.

VIOLET: I know they are, May. I know. But . . . well, can't you just love someone and leave it at that. Oh, I don't know. Love's a funny thing.

VIOLET *looks out of the window at* CHARLIE JUNIOR *and* CANNONBALL LEE.

VIOLET: Look at Charlie watching Dad. I sometimes think we forget all about Charlie.

MAY: He's as happy as a sandboy.

VIOLET (*calling*): Come on in for a cuppa, Dad. You'll catch your death of cold.

CANNONBALL (*calling back*): In a minute!

VIOLET: Charlie! You come and put your jumper on if you're going to stay out there.

CANNONBALL (*gently, at* CHARLIE): Go on, boy. Go in.

CHARLIE *comes in and gets a jumper. He is a good-looking boy, but lacks the menacing beauty that makes his twin brothers so alluring.*

VIOLET: What's he training for anyway, at his age. That's what I'd like to know.

HELEN: Christ knows. Want to make his own coffin probably. Silly old fool.

VIOLET: Oh, Mum. That's wicked.

HELEN: Wicked but true. Men are born children and they stay children. They scream and shout and boss people around – like your Father! – and they think they're in control.

CANNONBALL LEE *comes in from the back yard. He is an easy-going, jovial faced man, solidly built, and still*

strong-looking, even in old age. At any party, he'd be the
life and soul.

He walks through the parlour as quickly as possible to
escape his wife's moans.

HELEN (*calling after* CANNONBALL LEE): But they don't
know the half of it. Not half.

INT. ROSE'S HOUSE, LIVING ROOM. DAY
ROSE *is still polishing table, concerned about the scratches. The*
TWINS *are playing with their crocodiles.*

ROSE: This was your great-grandmother's table. Lovely
wood, walnut.

RON: We had a dream last night.

RON and REG: We had the same dream.

ROSE *looks down at the* TWINS. *She sees only magic in*
them, not menace.

ROSE: Tell me the dream.

RON: We dreamt we were standing in the street . . . and
suddenly . . . suddenly we started to rise up –

REG: – To fly –

RON: – We didn't have wings or anything . . . But we
flew –

REG: – You and Mum and Aunt May and Nanny, you were
all in the street . . . And you were watching us . . . And
we kept flying up and up –

RON: – We can't stop –

REG: – We just fly up –

RON: To the sun.

Something in ROSE *is moved by the story. Tears spring to*
her eyes. She goes to the window and looks out . . .
We see what she sees –

EXT. KRAY HOUSE. DAY

One of the houses has been hit by a bomb. Nothing but rubble remains. Its former occupants have not been daunted by the devastation. Like most East Enders during World War II, they must either look on the bright side or be consumed by the darkness. So the occupants (MAN, WOMAN, CHILD) are sitting in their ruined living room, in what is left of their sofa and armchairs, as if nothing has happened.

    MAN *is smoking a pipe and reading a newspaper. A* POLICEMAN *walks by. He is looking for something, someone . . . a certain house.*

POLICEMAN (*to the* MAN): You'll have to move now, won't you?

MAN (*laughing*): Why do you say that?

    POLICEMAN *laughs, then checks piece of paper he's holding.*

POLICEMAN: Do you know where Charlie Kray lives?

MAN: Charlie Kray. Yes – down there.

POLICEMAN: Thank you. Be lucky, you lot.

MAN: Luck? Never heard of it.

    POLICEMAN *walks towards the Kray house.*

POLICEMAN (*under his breath*): Alright, Charlie Kray. I've got you at last.

INT. ROSE'S HOUSE. DAY

ROSE *snaps into action.*

ROSE: Come on, boys!

RON and REG: What?

ROSE: No arguments! Come on!

    She starts shepherding the TWINS *out of the living room, and –*

EXT. KRAY HOUSE. DAY

– *out of her house.* ROSE *pushes the* TWINS *into* VIOLET'S *house.*

ROSE: Get inside! Warn your mum. I'll keep the miserable old bastard talking.

> *The* POLICEMAN *approaches the house.* ROSE *picks up doormat and flicks it in his face. Dust goes in* POLICEMAN'S *eyes.*

POLICEMAN: Ahh! Watch what you're doing!

INT. KRAY HOUSE, LIVING ROOM. DAY

CHARLIE SENIOR *is still asleep in his chair. Suddenly* VIOLET, HELEN *and* MAY *rush in* –

VIOLET: Wake!
HELEN: Quickly!
MAY: Up!
HELEN: Copper!
VIOLET: Cellar!

> CHARLIE, *startled, wakes and is rushed out of the room and* –

INT. KRAY HOUSE, HALLWAY. DAY

– *shoved down the hallway and into the cupboard beneath the stairs by* VIOLET, HELEN *and* MAY.

EXT. KRAY HOUSE. DAY

ROSE *is still distracting the* POLICEMAN.

> *Some people look over. One is the* NEIGHBOUR *we saw cleaning her doorstep earlier.*

NEIGHBOUR: Having trouble?
ROSE: Mind your own.

22

POLICEMAN: Yeah. Shove off.

ROSE (*to* POLICEMAN): You can shove off too.

POLICEMAN: Don't pester me, Rosie. There's a good girl.

ROSE: Don't bloody 'good girl' me! Who do you think
 you're talking to?

INT. KRAY HOUSE, HALLWAY. DAY

HELEN *is rushing towards front door, holding a milk bottle.*
MAY *follows.*

EXT. KRAY HOUSE. DAY

POLICEMAN *is still trying to push past* ROSE *to get into the
house.*

POLICEMAN: I'm just doing my job, Rosie.

ROSE: Who says?

POLICEMAN: Rosie! Come on now –
 HELEN *and* MAY *come out.* HELEN *drops milk bottle in
 front of* POLICEMAN – *blocking his entry.*

HELEN: What a mess! May!

MAY: A broom!

HELEN: And a mop and bucket. A woman's work is never
 done, Constable.

ROSE: Bloody mess.
 POLICEMAN *undeterred, makes his way into* VIOLET's
 house, and –

INT. KRAY HOUSE, HALLWAY. DAY

– *walks down hallway.*
 Suddenly POLICEMAN *falls over a broomstick.* VIOLET
appears with RON *and* REG *standing beside her.*

VIOLET: What's all this palaver?

23

POLICEMAN (*holding broom*): That's a lethal weapon, that is!

VIOLET: Housework is a lethal business, Constable.

POLICEMAN: I'm looking for your husband, Violet.

VIOLET: Well, when you find him, let me know. I've got three hungry mouths here need feeding.

POLICEMAN *looks at* RON, REG *and* CHARLIE. RON *and* REG *stare back with icy hatred.* POLICEMAN *visibly flinches from the* TWINS' *glare. He starts looking round the house.*

POLICEMAN: He's here somewhere, Violet. I know it. You can't fool me. Now where . . .

POLICEMAN *heads for the coal cellar beneath stairs . . .*

INT. KRAY HOUSE, COAL CELLAR. DAY

CHARLIE SENIOR *is hiding amongst the coal. His face is grimey with sweat. He nervously listens as the* POLICEMAN *gets closer . . .*

INT. KRAY HOUSE, HALLWAY. DAY

POLICEMAN: He should be out there fighting like everyone else, Violet. Fighting for his country. Not hiding like a –

POLICEMAN'*s hand is on the cellar door.*

RON: Our Dad's not an idiot!

POLICEMAN *stops, looks at* RON.

RON: Wouldn't hide in coal cupboard.

REG: Would he?

POLICEMAN *stares at them for a while.*

There's something hypnotic about their stare. Something irresistible. Something that tells POLICEMAN *it would be futile to continue his search.*

POLICEMAN: Oh well, never mind. I'll get him one day.

POLICEMAN *leaves the house.* VIOLET *opens the coal cellar door.*

VIOLET (*at* CHARLIE SENIOR): Get out, you!

    CHARLIE *clambers out, filthy, treading soot everywhere.*

VIOLET: Oh, look at you! The mess. Ron, get the bath out. Reg, start heating the water.

HELEN: I'll get the soap.

ROSE: And flannel.

MAY: And scrubbing brush.

    VIOLET *is so irritated she's near tears.*

VIOLET: Mess! All this mess. Just when everything was so tidy! Mess!

EXT. STREET WITH BAKER SHOP. DAY

A long queue is waiting for bread. Outside a baker shop. Everyone in queue is clutching ration tokens. The queue moves very slowly.

    ROSE *is in the middle of the queue.* RON *and* REG *play with their crocodiles on the pavement nearby. Two women are talking inanely in front of* ROSE. RON *and* REG *start to argue.*

RON (*indicating crocodile*): Give me yours.

REG: No.

RON: I want it.

REG: No. It's mine.

RON: Give it! Give it!

REG (*shouting*): No! No! No!

RON (*shrieking*): I want it!

ROSE: Hey, what's going on? Stop it, you two.

REG: He wants my crocodile.

ROSE: Why, Ron. You've got your own.

RON: His is better.

ROSE: It's not, luv. They're identical.

RON: It's not! I want it!

ROSE: Oh, stop arguing. There's good boys. Please. Your
Aunt Rose has got enough to contend with as it is.

RON *and* REG *calm down and start playing.*

ROSE *continues listening to the two women talk in front
of her. This is obviously a main part of what she's having
to contend with.*

FIRST WOMAN: I was going to get a bit of liver.

SECOND WOMAN: Oooo, I like liver.

FIRST WOMAN: Well, me too. Can't beat it, I say. But Jack!
He won't have it.

SECOND WOMAN: No?

FIRST WOMAN: Not a mouthful. A distant uncle of his had a
nasty accident with pipes once. In the liver.

SECOND WOMAN: Oooo, they can be nasty.

FIRST WOMAN: Fatal more like!

SECOND WOMAN: No!

FIRST WOMAN: Choked to death.

SECOND WOMAN: On liver?

FIRST WOMAN: On liver!

ROSE *can't take it any more . . .*

ROSE (*under her breath*): Oh, the crap people talk.

FIRST WOMAN: I heard that.

ROSE: You were meant to.

SECOND WOMAN: Rude cow! What you staring at?

ROSE: I don't know, but it's staring back.

SECOND WOMAN: Oooo, you bitch.

ROSE *punches* SECOND WOMAN. *It's a hard, vicious
punch, not a slap.*

It's meant to do harm. And it does! The SECOND
WOMAN *falls to the ground.*

FIRST WOMAN *jumps on* ROSE'S *back.* ROSE *claws at
her.* SECOND WOMAN *gets up.* ROSE *kicks her. She's on
the ground again.*

*The crowd part as the fight continues. And it's a vicious
one!*

Punching!

Clawing!

Kicking!

But, even though it's one against two, ROSE *is
undeniably winning. She's fighting in a way undreamt of
by the other two women. A viciousness the others could
never match.*

RON *and* REG *watch, fascinated, horrified, gripped,
clutching their crocodiles. Finally, the fight finishes. The
two women are in the gutter, bloody and unconscious.*

ROSE, *a little dishevelled, but otherwise unharmed,
smiles at* RON *and* REG. *She straightens her hair and
brushes down her clothes. Suddenly, it's as if she hadn't
been in a fight at all. If anything, she looks more relaxed
and content than earlier.*

The crowd parts for ROSE *to go into the shop.*

ROSE: Let's get some bread, boys.

ROSE, RON *and* REG *go into the shop.*

INT. BETHNAL GREEN TUBE. NIGHT

People sheltering from air-raid.

Noises of bombing from above.

Children crying.

Most people however are sitting round CANNONBALL LEE
*as he captivates them with his stories. He is a born story-teller.
You can tell by the faces of his audience that they are
mesmerised, have forgotten about the bombing.*

Golden lamplight flickers over their faces.

CANNONBALL LEE: . . . and then there was Blind Bill. He
could smell a copper from twenty paces. Nose like a dog
he had. In the end, he was stabbed in the neck. Walked
all the way from Aldgate to Mile End. Left a trail of
blood four miles long. And you know something, those

stains are still there today. Nothing can get rid of them; not wind, not snow, not human washing. My old Mum took me to see bloodstains once. Underneath the arches. Where Jack the Ripper cut up his victims. He cut them from here . . . (*Points at groin.*) . . . to here . . . (*Runs finger up to his throat.*) . . . gutted them like a fish.

MAY: He makes it sound so bloody glamorous.

CANNONBALL LEE: It's true. My old Mum saw him once too. Jack the Ripper. Saw him with her own eyes down Brick Lane. Tall he was, dressed in a long black cloak. His face was as white as chalk. Teeth sharp as tiny razors. And his eyes . . . Oooo . . . his eyes. Red they were! Bright red! Glowed like stars. My Mum was only a girl when she saw him but she went grey that night. He drained the colour from her hair . . .

The TWINS *are listening to the story, riveted. Violence, blood, magic, murder – it's the* TWINS' *perfect fairytale. And, like all good fairytales, it unlocks something within them. Some secret. Darkness calls to darkness . . .*

Suddenly, a bomb drops above.

The walls shake.

Dust falls from the ceiling.

RON *and* REG *rush to* VIOLET *for comfort. She wraps her arms around them. Her embrace feels safer than the deepest air-raid shelter.*

VIOLET: It's alright, my darlings. No-one's going to hurt you. Not with me around. They wouldn't dare. They wouldn't bloody dare.

INT. SCHOOL ROOM, 1944. DAY
It is a typical wartime classroom: stark, impersonal, heartless. Order, not education, the most important thing. At a quick glance, you'd mistake it for a prison or army barracks.

RON *and* REG *are sitting next to each other. They are older now, about eleven or twelve, on the brink of adulthood. There is something that separates them from the rest of the class. Something that says: Our rules are not your rules: In any battle, you would never win.*

One BOY *in the class is playing with a gasmask. A* TEACHER — *a grey man in late middle age — is pacing the classroom. He talks with an exaggerated military air, a hair's breadth from madness.*

TEACHER: Words! Words are rich and wonderful. We can say anything we like. Words get into your skin. They are like an illness. They can infect you. Words are a disease. But a wonderful disease. A disease without a cure. Words are weapons. And we must use them carefully.

The BOY *has put his gasmask on and is giggling.*

TEACHER *sees him.*

TEACHER (*angrily*): Boy!

TEACHER *rushes* BOY *and grabs him violently by ear.*

TEACHER: Come on, boy! Give me a wonderful word!

BOY (*painfully*): Sir?

TEACHER: Come on! There's millions to choose from. Tell me a wonderful word.

BOY: . . . Mum?

The class laughs. But not RON *and* REG.

TEACHER (*at class*): Quiet!

Instant silence!

TEACHER (*at* BOY): Mum! Mum might be wonderful to you. Not to me . . . You idiot!

TEACHER *releases the* BOY *and starts pacing the classroom.*

TEACHER: Alright . . . who else? Who else can give me a wonderful word? My whole body yearns for a

wonderful word . . . Krays! Save my life! Give me a
wonderful word.

REG *and* RON *stand, and immediately, boldly –*

RON and REG: Crocodile!

TEACHER: Crocodile! Yes . . . they might be wonderful.
Right. Ronald! Choose a poem and read it to us in your
velvet tones.

TEACHER *hands* RON *a book of poetry.*

RON: What poem, sir?

TEACHER: Any, boy, just read.

RON *opens the book at random and –*

RON (*falteringly*): 'From childhood's hour . . . I have not
been . . .

As . . . oth . . . others were . . . I have not seen . . .

As others saw. I could not bring

My passion from a common spring.

From the same source I have not taken

My sorrow: I could not awaken

My heart to joy at the same tone

And all I loved I loved alone . . .'

EXT. SCHOOL PLAYGROUND, 1994. DAY

RON *and* REG *are walking across the yard. The yard is full of
boys. Some boys back out of the way – the* TWINS *are obviously
the 'bullies' of the school.*

We continue hearing RON *read the poem, but the voice
changes . . .*

It gradually becomes an adult voice. The child RON, *becomes
adult* RON –

RON (*voice over*): 'Then in my childhood, in the dawn
Of a most stormy life – was drawn
From every depth of good and ill
The mystery which binds me still . . .'

Out of nowhere – and for no apparent reason – the TWINS
manufacture a fight.

RON (*voice over*): 'From the torrent, or the fountain,
From the red cliff of the mountain,
From the sun that round me rolled
In its autumn tint of gold . . .'
*They start hitting a boy. He fights back. Other boys join
in . . .*

> *There is a massive, violent 'tumble' of a fight. But the*
> TWINS *are obviously winning.*

RON (*voice over*): 'From the lightning in the sky
As it passed me flying by,
From the thunder and the storm . . .'
There is a vicious, cruel, bloody streak to the TWINS' *way
of fighting. A sadistic glee that is not apparent in any of
the other boys.*

RON (*voice over*): 'And the cloud that took the form
(when rest of Heaven was blue)'
When the fight is over, the other boys back away from the
TWINS. *They're afraid of the* TWINS.

> *The* TWINS *are left alone in the centre of the
> playground.*

RON (*voice over*): 'Of a demon in my view.'

INT. CHAMBER OF HORRORS TENT, 1951. DAY
We see dead Siamese twins.

They are floating in murky liquid.

*The Siamese twins are joined at the waist and are not fully
formed, foetal.*

*We are in a fairground tent. It is obviously a sort of freak
show or 'Chamber of Horrors'.* RON *and* REG *are looking at the
foetal Siamese twins. They are fascinated by the sight, a
horrified wonder.*

32

The TWINS *are in their late teens now, still angelic demons, though perhaps more menacing than magical now. Of the two,* RON *has the edge. There's a spiteful glint to his eye that's missing from* REG.

CHARLIE JUNIOR *is with the* TWINS, *as are several friends:* TERRY, EDDIE, DENNIS, TIMMY. *They are all roughly the same age, late teens, with clothes that look the worse for wear. If* RON *and* REG *are natural leaders, then these boys are born followers. They are all staring into jar.*

RON: What would have happened if they lived?

REG: That couldn't have lived.

TERRY (*giggling*): One eats and the food goes into the other's belly.

TERRY *offers* DENNIS *his bag of sweets.*

DENNIS (*pushing the bag away*): Oh no . . . I couldn't eat now –

EDDIE: It must be first bloody time –

DENNIS: Shut it, Eddie! And stop all that scratching. You're making me bloody itch.

TIMMY: Just think of it. Stuck to each other like that. Living and joined together. They're better dead.

REG: They should have been burned. It's not right somehow. Everyone gawking at them.

CHARLIE JUNIOR: Just like us!

RON: I think they look great.

REG *pulls* RON *away from the foetal exhibit and out of the tent. The others follow and they all –*

EXT. VICTORIA PARK FAIR. DAY

– *look around the fair.*

Ghost train.

Boxing tent.

Everyone laughing and enjoying themselves.

33

HELEN, VIOLET, MAY *and* ROSE *are standing round eating some candy. They're looking visibly older now, greyer, but still a formidable quartet.*

The TWINS, CHARLIE JUNIOR *and their friends walk by.*

RON: Hello, Mum.

VIOLET: Hello, darling.

REG: You alright, Gran?

HELEN: Not so bad, luv.

The TWINS, CHARLIE JUNIOR *walk towards the boxing tent . . .*

VIOLET: Oh, look, Mum, there's Mrs – oh, what's her name?

HELEN: Mrs East, luv.

VIOLET: That's right. Mrs East. Her daughter lost a leg in the war, didn't she?

HELEN: Deirdre, yes.

ROSE: Deirdre East! I've heard about her.

MAY: Oh, me too.

ROSE: They say her false leg's been propped in more bedrooms than I've had hot dinners.

HELEN: Oh, don't Rose.

ROSE: It's true, Mum.

VIOLET: It's wicked.

CANNONBALL LEE *comes up. He is obviously drunk. A few friends are with him.* CANNONBALL *is punching the air as if shadow boxing.*

CANNONBALL LEE (*at* HELEN): Want to come and see some boxing, old girl?

HELEN: No. And don't you 'old girl' me. Oh, your breath. It stinks. Really.

CANONBALL LEE: Come on, boys. Let's go and show 'em how to box. I've been training.

CANNONBALL *and friends head for the boxing tent . . .*

34

INT. BOXING TENT. DAY

A make-shift ring is set up in the middle of the tent.

   A rowdy, and predominantly male, crowd surround the ring.
Air thick with smoke.

   In the ring a REFEREE *is introducing the champion –* THE
COCKNEY DEVIL *– (a huge, bulldog of a man, and just as*
hairy) to the audience.

REFEREE: Anyone who can go three rounds with The
     Cockney Devil here wins . . . not ten bob, not fifteen
     bob, not even eighteen bob – but a quid. A whole quid!
     So . . . come on. Who's going to be brave enough?

     CANNONBALL LEE *has pushed his way through the*
     crowd and is now clambering into the ring.

      RON, REG, CHARLIE JUNIOR *and their friends*
     congregate nearby.

      CANNONBALL LEE *sits in his corner.* REFEREE *comes*
     up to CANNONBALL LEE.

REFEREE: What's your name?

CANNONBALL LEE: Cannonball Lee!

REFEREE: Cannonball Lee. You know the rules. Stay three
     rounds and you get a quid.

     CHARLIE JUNIOR *is obviously worried.* CANNONBALL
     LEE *looks puny – and so very, very old – beside the tower*
     of aggressive muscle that is THE COCKNEY DEVIL.

      CHARLIE JUNIOR *tries to attract* CANNONBALL
     LEE*'s attention, persuading him to leave the ring.*

     CANNONBALL *will have none of it.*

CHARLIE JUNIOR: Grandad! What you doing? You're too
     old. Get out of there! Pack it in!

CANNONBALL LEE: I'll tear his bloody head off.

REFEREE: Ladies and gentlemen! Cannonball Lee!

     CANNONBALL *comes to the centre of the ring.* THE
     COCKNEY DEVIL *faces him. For a moment they stare at*
     each other. THE COCKNEY DEVIL *plays with*

CANNONBALL LEE. CANNONBALL LEE *is obviously out of his class.*

AUDIENCE (*chanting*): Cannonball! Cannonball! Cannonball!

THE COCKNEY DEVIL *plays with* CANNONBALL *some more.*

CHARLIE JUNIOR: Get out, Grandad! (*At* RON.) We've got to get him out. This is stupid.

RON (*flatly*): Leave him.

CHARLIE JUNIOR: He'll be slaughtered.

RON: Leave him.

Suddenly, in the ring, CANNONBALL LEE *gets a lucky punch through. It strikes* THE COCKNEY DEVIL *in the jaw.* THE COCKNEY DEVIL'*s more surprised than hurt.* CANNONBALL LEE *raises his fists in triumph.*

The audience cheers.

THE COCKNEY DEVIL, *irritated, and with a look that says 'playtime's over', strides forward and gives* CANNONBALL LEE *a solid punch in the stomach.* CANNONBALL LEE *hangs over the ropes and throws up over the man ringing the bell.*

The contest is over. CANNONBALL LEE *is taken from the ring.*

RON *and* REG *look at each other. Instinctively,* REG *reaches out to take* RON'*s jacket as he takes it off. They smile at each other.* RON *gets into the ring. He sits in corner and starts taking off his shirt. The* REFEREE *goes to* RON . . .

REFEREE: What's your name?

RON: Ronnie Kray.

REFEREE: Where you from?

RON: Bethnal Green.

REFEREE (*to audience*): Ronnie Kray from Bethnal Green.

RON *glares at* THE COCKNEY DEVIL. *This is obviously no game.*

THE COCKNEY DEVIL *starts to play with* RON *in the same way he did with* CANNONBALL LEE. RON *is tense as a panther, his eyes glaring. Finally,* THE COCKNEY DEVIL *gives* RON *a punch. It is hard. Hits him on the jaw . . .*

The punch transforms RON. *We can see the change in his face. It brings out the monster inside.* RON's *eyes flare, his face becomes a grimace. He is wild with anger. He gives* THE COCKNEY DEVIL *a punch in the stomach, one to the jaw, another in the stomach.*

RON *drives* THE COCKNEY DEVIL *back . . . back . . . Punch! Punch! Punch!*

THE COCKNEY DEVIL's *nose explodes, his lip bursts . . .*

Punch! Punch! Punch!

THE COCKNEY DEVIL *collapses.*

There is a moment's shocked silence. Up till now it had all been quite a playful little game. RON *has changed it. In the audience* REG *starts cheering and clapping, followed by his friends. In the ring, the* REFEREE *holds up* RON's *arm, albeit a bit warily.*

REFEREE: The winner!

The rest of the audience cheers, again . . . warily.

REFEREE: Now come on ladies and gentlemen . . . Who's next? Who'll take on this young man?

The audience shuffles uneasily. A few move away.

RON *looks at* REG.

REG *looks at* RON.

Then . . . REG *goes to get in the ring.* CHARLIE JUNIOR *goes to stop him.*

CHARLIE JUNIOR: Reg! What you doing Reg! No!

REG: Leave me!

CHARLIE JUNIOR: But you can't.

REG: Leave me!

38

CHARLIE JUNIOR *lets him go.* REG *climbs into the ring, smiling.* RON *smiles back.*

REFEREE (*at* REG): What's your name?

REG: Reggie Kray.

REFEREE: Reggie Kray! Ronnie Kray. Look at you! You're brothers! Twins!

RON/REG (*smiling*): Yeah.

REFEREE: Ladies and gentlemen! The Kray Twins!

The TWINS *begin their fight. And what a fight. There is no messing between them. Both are out to win, both are as good as each other, neither one will give in first. With each punch, there is blood.*

Punch . . . blood.

Punch!

Blood!

And the sight of blood goads the TWINS *on. To more and more frenzy.*

Punch! Punch! Blood!

The REFEREE *tries to stop it, but the* TWINS *won't let him in.*

Blood! Blood! Blood!

The audience are shocked. No-one is cheering. This is no longer a carnival: It's a nightmare. CHARLIE JUNIOR *can take it no more. He rushes out of the tent . . . and –*

EXT. VICTORIA PARK FAIR. DAY
– runs through crowd towards VIOLET.

CHARLIE JUNIOR (*urgently*): Mum! Mum!

VIOLET: What, luv?

CHARLIE JUNIOR: Quick!

CHARLIE JUNIOR *pulls* VIOLET *towards the boxing tent.*

39

INT. BOXING TENT. DAY

The fight between RON *and* REG *is continuing . . . The
savagery is intensifying. Both their faces are covered in blood.*
  Blood! Blood!

  VIOLET *runs into the tent with* CHARLIE JUNIOR. *She sees
what's happening in the ring and gasps in horror.*

VIOLET: No!
  She rushes to the ring.
VIOLET: Ron! Reg! Stop it!
  VIOLET *pushes herself between* RON *and* REG *to stop the
  fighting.*
VIOLET: Stop! Stop! Stop!
  RON *and* REG *stop the fighting. They look at* VIOLET,
  dripping blood.

INT. KRAY HOUSE, LIVING ROOM. DAY

RON *is having his wounds bathed by* AUNT ROSE. REG *by*
MAY. HELEN *is putting a plaster on* CANNONBALL LEE*'s
forehead.* VIOLET *is sitting by the table. She is obviously very
upset.*

VIOLET: When you were born . . . when I held you in my
  arms, I thought, 'There will be no hurt. I have my boys
  to protect me. Look after me . . .'
CHARLIE JUNIOR: Don't, Mum –
VIOLET: Don't tell me, don't. What have we got? All of us?
  Nothing. Except each other. God in heaven, I never
  thought I'd see . . . (*She spins on* CANNONBALL LEE.)
  This is all your bloody fault.
CANNONBALL LEE: I thought they were very good.
HELEN: For once in your life know when to shut up.
CANNONBALL LEE: I thought it was a bloody good fight.

40

VIOLET (*talking through her tears*): Fight? Fight? I'll tell you
what fighting is! Fighting is bringing up three kids
through the war on hardly enough food to feed a cat on.
That's what fighting is. And now you're telling me I've
done all that to have my heart broken like this . . .
Broken . . .

MAY: Oh, Vi . . . Come on!

VIOLET goes to RON *and* REG. *She kneels in front of*
them. RON *and* REG *have their heads bowed, too ashamed*
to meet VIOLET's *look.*

VIOLET: Listen to me. We don't fight each other. We stick
together. That's how we're strong. If you want something . . . yes . . . you fight to get it. Like I fight, like
mum fights . . . Fight them out there . . . But we don't
fight each other . . . Not for fun . . . Not for no money
. . . Not for no reason . . . You hear me? We never fight
each other.

Now RON *and* REG *look up. They each take one of*
VIOLET's *hands and kiss it.*

RON: We're sorry, Mum.

REG: We're sorry, Mum.

VIOLET starts to stroke their hair.

VIOLET: You're me world, you two. You mean everything
to me. Don't spoil it . . .

EXT. KRAY HOUSE. DAY
VIOLET is cleaning her windows. POSTMAN *cycles up.*

POSTMAN: Morning, Mrs Kray.

VIOLET: Morning.

POSTMAN hands VIOLET *two letters. She stares at them*
with thoughtful dread . . .

INT. KRAY HOUSE, LIVING ROOM. DAY

RON *and* REG *are looking at their respective letters.* CHARLIE SENIOR *is sitting at the table.* VIOLET *is pouring tea.*

VIOLET (*angrily*): Bloody National Service. What right have they got? No-one takes my boys away from me. No-one.

CHARLIE SENIOR: It'll do them good.

VIOLET: Oh, what do you know about it?

CHARLIE SENIOR: More than you think.

VIOLET: What?

CHARLIE SENIOR: Things.

VIOLET: Oh, things. I see. Things. Like how to hide from the police and fall asleep in that bloody armchair.

CHARLIE SENIOR: And what do you know, woman? You've been stuck in this house all your sodding life –

VIOLET: You listen to me, Charlie Kray! A house is a bloody battleground all by itself. I don't have to leave these four walls to see death and heartache. I've got it on my doorstep. And don't you dare preach to me. You've spent your whole life lying and cheating and what have you got to show for it? An armchair full of mothballs.

CHARLIE SENIOR *stands, angrily. It looks as if he is about to hit* VIOLET.

VIOLET: Go on. I dare you. Only if you do, you best kill me while you're at it because – on my mother's life – I'll slit your throat while you're sleeping. Charlie Kray, I swear I will.

CHARLIE SENIOR *takes an angry step forward, but –* REG *and* RON *stand up in unison. If they were dogs they'd be snarling.*

RON (*angrily*): Don't you dare touch Mum.

CHARLIE SENIOR: What?

REG: You heard. Just don't.

CHARLIE SENIOR *looks at* VIOLET *seeking help. None comes. He is bewildered. He cowers away from them, then becomes ashamed of his own fear.*

Within the story of the family, he knows he has faded away altogether . . .

INT. ARMY BARRACKS. DAY
Close up of SERGEANT. *He is a middle-aged man, moustached, aggressive: in other words, a military nightmare.*

SERGEANT: You are scum and slime, the best part of you crawled down your mother's legs when you were born, you're not men.
Slowly pull out to reveal him talking in the barracks. New recruits – in uniform – standing by beds.

REG *and* RON *stand opposite each other. Also there are* TERRY *and* PERRY. *As the* SERGEANT *speaks, it's obvious that* RON *and* REG *are bored by the whole thing. They could never take something like this seriously. For them, it can only be a joke.*

SERGEANT: You're not people anymore. You're not human beings. From now on you're part of a machine. You don't wear what you want to, think what you want to. You wear what we give you, think what we tell you, eat when we tell you, sleep, shit and fuck when we tell you.
REG *and* RON *roll their eyes at each other. They look across at* TERRY *who smiles but does not – like the* TWINS *– relax his position.*

DICKIE SMITH *is also smiling.* PERRY *can barely contain his giggles.*

The SERGEANT *spots him –*
SERGEANT: Someone stick a feather up your arse, lad?
PERRY: Sir?
SERGEANT: You're grinning like a bloody Cheshire Cat –

44

The SERGEANT *is interrupted as* REG *and* RON *casually walk past him towards the door. The* SERGEANT *is completely at a loss. His routine is broken.*

*REG *and* RON *reach the door.*

SERGEANT (*screaming*): And where do you think you little darlings are going?

RON (*casually*): Home!

REG: For a cuppa!

RON: With our Mum!

SERGEANT: Get your nasty little arses back here.

REG (*calmly*): Look, you've got nothing to say and you're saying it too loudly. So –

RON: – Bollocks!

The SERGEANT *stands with his mouth open. Giggling from the other men.*

SERGEANT: Quiet!

The dormitory quietens.

The TWINS *turn and open the door. The* SERGEANT *rushes to the* TWINS *and grabs* RON's *arm. Instantly,* RON *spins round and punches the* SERGEANT. *The* SERGEANT *falls to the floor with a crash.*

INT. DARK CELL. NIGHT

RON *and* REG *are laying on bunks. An older man is there with them. The man's name is* GEORGE.

Moonlight illuminates the scene, ethereal, unearthly. Voices are echoed, like they're in a cave.

GEORGE: I know your name. Kray. And I think to myself George, I think, these boys are special. These boys are a new kind. You've got it.

*REG *and* RON *are listening.* GEORGE's *voice is like the dark itself, whispering to them.*

GEORGE: You've got it. And I can see it. And you've got to
    learn how to use it . . . Now these people . . . they don't
    like getting hurt. Not them or their property. Now,
    these people out there who don't like to be hurt, pay
    other people not to hurt them. You know what I'm
    saying. Course you do. When you get out . . . you keep
    your eyes open . . . Watch out for the people who don't
    want to be hurt. Because you scare the shit out of me,
    boys. (*Pause.*) Wonderful.

INT. THE REGAL CLUB. NIGHT
It is late at night. REG *and* RON *are playing pool.* PERRY *is
talking to the* MANAGER. MANAGER *is a short fat man in his
late forties. On a nearby table two young men are finishing their
game.*

MANAGER: This place . . . I tell you, this place used to be so
    beautiful. There were chandeliers. Gold trimmings.
    Little cherubs with bunches of grapes.
    *The two young men finish their game. They go over to the
    nearby cloakroom.* MANAGER *goes over to give them their
    coats.*
MANAGER: Enjoy yourselves, lads?
FIRST YOUNG MAN: No.
MANAGER: That's good.
    *As the two young men leave, so five Italians walk in. They
    are dressed very smart. The kind of look that shrieks
    'Crook'.*
    RON *nods at* PERRY. PERRY *moves to door through
    which the Italians have just entered, blocking it.*
FIRST ITALIAN (*to* MANAGER): You're looking younger,
    Mr Willaby. What is it? A new aftershave perhaps?
MANAGER: You're early.
FIRST ITALIAN: A mere five minutes.

MANAGER: I haven't had time to count . . . it.

RON and REG are moving over to the cloakroom.

FIRST ITALIAN: Then count it!

RON (*to* MANAGER): Coat please . . . (*'Accidentally' knocks*
FIRST ITALIAN.) Oh, sorry mate. What's it like out?
Raining?

FIRST ITALIAN: Spitting.

RON: Bloody weather.

REG comes up.

REG (*at* MANAGER): Coat please . . .

RON: It's still spitting, Reg.

REG (*at* FIRST ITALIAN): That right, mate?

RON and REG are handed their coats. MANAGER *is now
nervously stuffing money into an envelope.*

FIRST ITALIAN: Not as bad as it was.

RON and REG are fiddling with the lining of their coats.

REG: We haven't got an umbrella, either.

RON: Always the way.

*The TWINS each produce a lethal looking sabre from the
lining of their coats. The silver glints.*

FIRST ITALIAN: Is this a joke?

RON: You see me laughing?

*FIRST ITALIAN laughs. RON lashes out with the blade. It
cuts FIRST ITALIAN's cheek.*

Suddenly the air is alive with gleaming silver.

*One makes a dash for the door but RON kicks it shut.
Another runs and REG's cutlass cuts across his back,
ripping through his coat, jacket, shirt, skin. The cutlasses
'whish' and 'sting' through the air. The TWINS are
ruthless in their attack. Once or twice it comes to fisticuffs,
but the TWINS are just as lethal with their fists as with
their blades.*

*The TWINS jump from snooker table to snooker table
. . . Cutlasses whip at the Italians.*

Cut through sleeves.

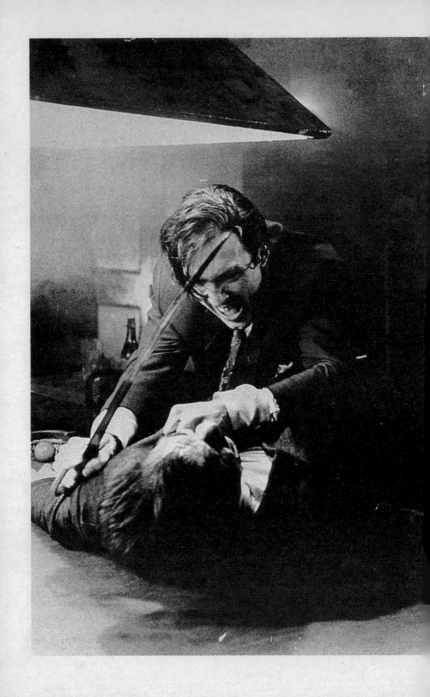

Trousers.

Skin . . .

The Italians are screaming, their blood covers the billiard tables as they try to make their escape.

Cut! Blood! Cut! Blood!

Three of the five are, by now, cut to ribbons, their clothes nothing more than shreds . . . But still the blades whish, thrust and cut.

Whish! Blood! Whish! Blood!

REG *closes in on the* FIRST ITALIAN.

Blood! Blood! Blood!

The FIRST ITALIAN *is lacerated severely about the face and hands.* REG *puts the point of the cutlass at his throat.*

REG: You go back. You tell everyone. Tell all of them. No-one fucks with us. This is nothing. Hold out your hand.

The FIRST ITALIAN *is shaking, hesitates.*

REG (*loudly*): Do it!

The FIRST ITALIAN *tentatively holds out his hand.* RON *stabs through the palm of the* FIRST ITALIAN*'s hand with his cutlass, he pins it to a billiard table.*

REG: Show them this. And say, we let you off lightly. Hear me?

The FIRST ITALIAN *goes to speak, but the pain is too severe. Tears of agony mingle with blood on his face.*

RON *twists the blade.*

The FIRST ITALIAN *screams.*

REG: Now say thank you!

The FIRST ITALIAN *musters all of his strength and through lips dripping blood, manages to whisper . . .*

REG: Say it.

FIRST ITALIAN: Th . . . thank . . . thank you . . .

Blood!

Blood!

Blood!

RON *and* REG *let* FIRST ITALIAN *fall to floor. He
starts crawling towards door.* RON *and* REG *walk over to
the* MANAGER. *He is trembling with fear.*

RON: How much this place cost you? When you first bought
it?

MANAGER: Five quid.

RON *grabs the box of money. Takes five quid and throws it
at the* MANAGER.

RON: You were robbed.

RON *and* REG *look round at the Regal. It's theirs now.
Their new home.*

Their eyes glint as viciously as the blooded blades . . .

RON: We'll get your little cherubs back.

INT. KRAY HOUSE, HALLWAY STAIRS. NIGHT
VIOLET *comes downstairs. She is wearing a very smart dress.
Fur round her shoulders, obviously going somewhere very
special. She goes into the living room where –*

INT. KRAY HOUSE, LIVING ROOM. NIGHT
– REG *and* RON *are looking in mirror. They are obviously
about to go out somewhere: very smartly dressed in black suits,
hair slick, everything about them seems to glint and sparkle.*

VIOLET *smiles when she sees the* TWINS.

VIOLET: . . . Look at you! Proper little gentlemen. You've
made me proud. The both of you. You've made it all
mean something.

RON: Oh, Mum –

VIOLET: It's true. Don't argue with your mother. (*Does a
twirl.*) How do I look?

RON: Lovely, Mum.

REG: Lovely, Mum.

51

VIOLET: You don't think it's a bit . . . well, you know. A bit mutton dressed up like lamb.

REG: You'll be the Princess of the ball . . .

VIOLET: Wicked Queen more like.

ROSE *comes in with a triumphant, 'Tra-la!' She too: fur, jewellery, hat with feather in, dressed for a special occasion.*

VIOLET: And here's the Fairy Godmother.

ROSE (*smiling*): The carriage awaits outside. Let's get it before it turns back into a pumpkin . . .

VIOLET: Look at 'em, Rose. What do they look like?

REG (*blushing*): Oh, stop it, Mum.

VIOLET: You're not shy in front of your Aunt Rose, are you?

RON: Oh, Mum . . .

VIOLET: Tell your Aunt Rose where you got the clothes. Go on. Tell her. Spit it out.

RON (*softly*): Savile Row.

ROSE: Savile Row!

VIOLET (*with pride*): Go on, Reg. Take off your jacket. Show your Aunt Rose the cut of your shirt . . .

REG: Ow, Mum –

VIOLET: Go on, I said.

REG *opens his jacket.*

VIOLET: And look at this, Rose. Look at this!

VIOLET *pulls* REG's *jacket even wider to reveal an embroidered 'KK' on the shirt pocket.*

VIOLET: Is that beautiful?

ROSE: Oh yes.

VIOLET: You know, Dad would have to work a whole year to own a shirt like that.

VIOLET *takes a step back to admire the* TWINS. *If she was any more full of pride, she'd burst.*

VIOLET: You must feel so proud when you're at your place. What do you feel like?

ROSE: Like kings?

RON/REG (*grinning*): Like kings!

EXT. THE REGAL. NIGHT
*It is obviously 'opening night' of 'THE REGAL'. Crowds
outside.*
  Bright lights. A few camera flashes going off –
  A black Mercedes pulls up. PERRY *is driving.* RON *and* REG
get out. Then help VIOLET *and* ROSE *out. As they're about to
enter* DENNIS *comes up.*

DENNIS (*at* VIOLET): Mrs Kray.
VIOLET: Hello, Den, luv.
  DENNIS *whispers something to* RON. RON*'s look hardens,
  then he nods.*
RON (*at* PERRY): Take me Mum and Aunt Rose in. Get
  them a drink.
PERRY: My pleasure, Ron.
VIOLET: Where you going?
RON: Back in a second, Mum. Enjoy yourself.
  RON *and* REG *rush off.*
VIOLET: Always on the move, you two are!

INT. THE REGAL, BALLROOM. NIGHT
*A large glitzy crowd has assembled. The air is full of smoke. A
band is playing.*
  *The whole Kray family is present: everyone having a good
time. We see* IRIS, CHARLIE JUNIOR*'s wife, for the first time
now.*
  *A dance has just finished. As it does so, one or two people try
to persuade* CANNONBALL LEE *to give them a song.*

CANNONBALL LEE: No . . . no . . .
HELEN: Go on, luv.
CANNONBALL LEE: Oh, I couldn't.

54

ROSE: You know you want to, Dad.

CANNONBALL LEE: Well . . .

MAY: Go on, Dad.

CANNONBALL LEE: Oh . . . alright then. Just one.

> *With an eagerness that belies his initial reluctance,* CANNONBALL LEE *rushes over to the* BANDMASTER *and whispers in his ear.* BANDMASTER *nods; yes, he knows that song. The band starts to play . . .* CANNON- BALL LEE *sings along, even giving a little dance as he does so . . .*

CANNONBALL LEE (*sings 'The Rogue in Vogue'*):

> I'm a Jack the Lad.
> And a bleeding crook.
> But I'm a dandy geezer
> In anyone's book.
>
> I dress up to the nines.
> Buy flowers for me Mum.
> Yes, I'm a little charmer.
> See how you all succumb.
>
> I'm the rogue in vogue
> With all the chaps.
> I'm the rogue in vogue:
> Watch girls collapse.
> I'll slip you a fiver.
> You'll be my friend for life.
> And if you're not then watch it!
> 'Cos I've got a gun and knife.
>
> Oh, I'm a one in a million.
> An ace! A gem! A king!
> I get away with right blue murder.
> And they say, one day, I'll swing.
>
> I'm the rogue in vogue
> With all the chaps.

I'm the rogue in vogue:
Watch girls collapse.
I'll slip you a fiver.
You'll be my friend for life.
And, if you're not, then watch it!
'Cos I've got a gun and knife.

I'm a handsome little devil.
No doubt I'll rot in hell.
Well, I won't mind that one bit
'Cos, folks, this life's been swell.

INT. KRAY'S OFFICE AT REGAL. NIGHT
DENNIS *is talking to the* TWINS. *He has two young boys with
him. Noises of Regal (*CANNONBALL LEE's *singing etc.)
muffled.*

DENNIS: . . . I said they should come here. They need a
    place, Reg. They've been on the run.
REG: Sure, sure. No trouble. You did right, Den.
RON: How old are you boys?
FIRST BOY: Fourteen, Mr Kray.
RON: You need some clothes and a hot meal, eh?
SECOND BOY: Yes, sir . . . we're starving.
    RON *takes his wallet out and hands the boys a wad of notes
    each.*
RON: Take this, get what you need. Clothes are important,
    make you what you are. Look after them, Den. Make
    sure they're safe.
DENNIS: Sure, come on boys.
    DENNIS *and the young boys leave.* REG *stares at* RON.
    A beat.
REG: Your tie's crooked.
RON: So is yours.

INT. THE REGAL, BALLROOM. NIGHT
A very theatrical spotlight on RON. *He is talking to the crowd.*

RON: Good evening, everybody. Welcome to our little club.
You all look marvellous. Really. You've done us proud.
Thank you.
There is a special eye contact between RON *and a guy in
the crowd. This is* STEVE — *he is young (about seventeen or
eighteen) — and very good looking.* STEVE *watches every
move* RON *makes.*

Several girls hang onto REG's *arm as he walks past
them. He shrugs them off with a smile.*

RON: But first I'd like to introduce you to the boss. The one
you can go to with all your troubles no matter how small
they are, he wants to help.
*The spotlight travels to a red curtain covering a doorway.
The men standing there open the curtain and — to
everyone's surprise — reveal a donkey! Applause and
clapping from the crowd.*

STEVE *comes over and puts his arm round* RON.
STEVE: This is great.
RON: I know.
STEVE: What a geezer you are.
RON's *happy, smiles at* STEVE, *relaxed. Then —* RON
looks up to see REG *talking to a girl. She is* FRANCES:
young, with a fragile, painfully innocent beauty.

RON's *joyous expression instantly changes. It becomes a
jealous stare. If looks could kill, the guests would be
scraping* FRANCES *off the floor.*
STEVE *(at* RON*):* What is it? What —
RON *pushes* STEVE *off. Then — he spins on a man in the
crowd. The man had been minding his own business, but
that doesn't matter to* RON —
RON: What did you say?
MAN *(nervously):* Me? Why . . . nothing.

58

RON: Yes you did. You called me something. What did you
    call me?

MAN: Nothing. Honestly. I didn't say a word.

RON (*shaking with rage*): You called me a boy.

MAN: I didn't say nothing.

> RON *walks over to him, grabs him by the lapels. The man*
> *cries out, petrified.*

RON: You wanker. Is all this the work of a boy? God
    Almighty. Boy! Boy! Boy!

> RON *pushes man out of ballroom, followed by the others.*
>> REG *notices the fight brewing. He excuses himself from*
> FRANCES . . .

EXT. ALLEY AT BACK OF REGAL. NIGHT
Neon lights.
  Dustbins.
  Shadows.
  And more shadows . . .

> RON *pushes man out of back door of the Regal and into*
> *alleyway. The man stumbles to the ground, trembling with fear.*
> REG, STEVE, PERRY, DENNIS *and some other men follow*
> RON, *with the expectations of a crowd awaiting a bullfight.*
> RON *takes his jacket off, preparing for a scrap. The man, in*
> *desperation, takes a small blade from his pocket.*
>> STEVE *goes to help* RON. REG *pulls* STEVE *back.*

REG: Leave him!

> *The man faces* RON *with the blade.* RON *laughs.*

RON: You stupid sod . . . Go on then, cut me.

> *The man hesitates.*

MAN: Look. I don't want any trouble . . . I . . .

RON: Go on. Cut me. You haven't got the guts.

> RON *rips open his shirt, lays it bare, inviting the blade.*

59

RON: Go on! Cut me! Cut me! Go on . . . (RON *relaxes, smiles at man.*) See. No need for violence. Stupid. Why act like kids? Come on. Let's forget the whole thing.
The man relaxes a little, discards the knife.

RON: That's better . . . Don't want to go round threatening people with piddly little knives like that, do you? Not when I've got a knife as well . . .
RON – *as if by magic – produces a sabre.*

MAN: No! . . . Please! No!
RON *closes in on the man. He pushes him violently against the wall.*

RON: Laugh at me, eh? I'm going to make you laugh for the rest of your fucking life!

MAN: Ronnie! Why are you doing this to me?
RON *raises the sabre . . .*
He pushes it, horizontally, across the man's mouth. The man screams.
RON *pushes the sabre . . .*
It cuts into the man's face, through his cheeks. The man's shrieks of pain gargle with blood . . .

INT. REGAL, WASHROOMS. NIGHT
RON *has his jacket and shirt off and is washing his hands. The water in the sink is scarlet.* STEVE *is helping* RON *on with a new shirt.*

STEVE: You scared me.

RON: I can take care of myself. Why don't you go back to the party. Talk to the donkey.
STEVE *comes and puts his arm round* RON, *kisses him full on the mouth.*

STEVE: You made a mess of his face.

RON: They scooped up enough to put it back together. (*Sniffs.*) What you wearing?

STEVE: I don't know, why?

RON: I don't like it. Change it. And those shoes are wrong.

STEVE: Well, you bought them.

RON: Well, I'll have to buy you some more, won't I?

> REG *enters.* RON *signals for* STEVE *to leave. He does so.* REG *comes in and leans against the mirror.* RON *pulls a comb from his pocket and runs it through his hair.*

REG: I want to get Mum something.

RON: We get her lots of things. You know how she carries on. Don't spend your money on me, spend it on yourself.

REG: I know. But she needs something to keep her company. Now that we're not there so much.

RON: I'm there when I can. (*Sees bloodstain on collar.*) Bloody hell, this is a new shirt.

REG: That's not going to notice with your jacket on.

RON: Remind me to give it to Aunt May to wash. You know . . . I had my perfect dream last night.

REG: What's that?

RON: That I was asleep in bed and I looked like you.

> *They embrace. Then* RON *puts his jacket on.* REG *goes to the door, waiting for him.* RON *looks at the bloodstain on the collar again.*

RON: Sodding bloodstains. They do show.

REG: So what shall we get Mum?

INT. KRAY HOUSE, LIVING ROOM. DAY

VIOLET, HELEN, ROSE *and* IRIS *are all looking at the new television set. It's in the corner of the room. This, obviously, is the* TWINS' *gift.*

HELEN: It's very big. Don't you think? After all, most of the time it just sits there.

VIOLET: Reg says everyone'll have one soon.

IRIS: Charlie says the same thing.
ROSE: When does it come on, then?
MAY: When it gets darker, I suppose.
ALL: Mmmm . . .

EXT. FRANCES LAWSON'S HOUSE, STREET. DAY
A sparkling, green Daimler drives down a street. In the back seat is REG. *He is dressed immaculately in black and holding a bunch of flowers.* TERRY *sits next to him.* GREY *is driving.*
  The car stops outside a terraced house we have not seen before. REG *gets out of the car and walks towards the house . . .*

INT. FRANCES LAWSON'S HOUSE, FRONT ROOM. DAY
MRS LAWSON *is peeking through the curtains. She is in her mid-forties, and obviously wearing her Sunday best. To say she appears mousy is an understatement: a good sneeze might finish her off for good.*
  MR LAWSON *is slouched in his favourite armchair. He is dressed casually, reading a newspaper. He might not be stronger than his wife, but he's more opinionated, more entrenched in his views. In other words: a pig-headed mouse.*

MRS LAWSON: Nice car. Green. Brought flowers too.
  MR LAWSON *grunts, discontent, from behind his newspaper.*
MRS LAWSON (*glancing at him*): You can't just sit there and make out it's not happening, you know.
MR LAWSON: Can do what I like in my own house.
MRS LAWSON: You've got to make an effort. For Frances' sake.
  The doorbell rings.
MRS LAWSON: Frank! Let him in! I'll get Frances.
  MR LAWSON *doesn't move.*
MRS LAWSON: Frank!

63

No movement.

MRS LAWSON: Frank! Please!

MR LAWSON: Just don't expect me to talk to him. I didn't
fight in the war for the likes of him . . .

> MR LAWSON *goes to answer the door.* MRS LAWSON *goes*
> *upstairs.*

INT. FRANCES LAWSON'S HOUSE, FRANCES' BEDROOM. DAY

FRANCES *is wearing her slip, staring at several dresses strewn*
across the bed. There are clothes scattered everywhere: we get
the feeling she's been trying her entire wardrobe on all day.

> FRANCES *is just as beautiful as when we saw her in the*
> *Regal, only now there's something else. A radiance to her. A*
> *joy. Someone in love.*

> MRS LAWSON *enters.*

MRS LAWSON: Reg is downstairs.

FRANCES: What dress, Mum?

> FRANCES *picks up two of the dresses from the bed: a*
> *yellow one and a blue one.*

MRS LAWSON: Oh, I don't know –

FRANCES: What one?

MRS LAWSON: Oh . . . the blue.

FRANCES: No. The yellow one.

MRS LAWSON: Why ask me if you know. Now come
downstairs.

FRANCES: What does he look like? Handsome, eh?

MRS LAWSON: Oh, yes, certainly handsome.

FRANCES: I told you. Prince Charming.

> FRANCES *struggles into the blue dress.*

INT. FRANCES LAWSON'S HOUSE, SITTING ROOM. DAY

REG, FRANCES, MR LAWSON *and* MRS LAWSON *are sitting*
with bone china cups and saucers balanced on their laps. MRS

64

LAWSON *is talking. She is doing so relentlessly to cover up for* MR LAWSON, *who is glaring at* REG.

It would take a chainsaw – not a knife – to make a dent in this atmosphere.

MRS LAWSON *cuts the cake, hands it out, and no-one is quite sure where to put the tea and various plates.*

REG: Nice cake.

MRS LAWSON: Oh thanks, Reg . . . I've always thought it'd be nice to bake my own cakes but, really, there isn't the time. Though, Frank would like me to. Wouldn't you, Frank?

MR LAWSON: All the same to me. Cakes is cakes.

MRS LAWSON: Oh, well, that isn't what he keeps saying to me. You see, Frank's mother was a great cake maker. But she kept her own hens so she was halfway there –

MR LAWSON (*at* REG): What's your job?

FRANCES: I told you, Dad. Reg owns some clubs.

MR LAWSON: Must pay well. To have a car like that.

REG: Keeps me comfortable, Mr Lawson.

MRS LAWSON: More cake, Reg?

FRANCES (*standing*): Oh, for God's sake! He doesn't want anymore cake. Shall we go outside, Reg?

REG *and* FRANCES *leave and go out to the –*

EXT. LAWSON'S HOUSE, BACK GARDEN. DAY
– arm in arm.

FRANCES: Reg, I'm sorry.

REG: Don't be. Natural for a dad to make sure his daughter can be looked after. Natural. (*Looks round.*) You've got a lovely garden. (*Goes to rose bush.*) Nice roses. My Mum loves roses.

65

REG *takes a small black box from his pocket. He hands it
to* FRANCES.

FRANCES: What is it?

REG: A present . . . Well, open it.

> FRANCES *opens the box. Inside we see a small silver
> brooch.*
>
> > *It's in the shape of a crocodile.*
> > *It glints in the sunlight.*

FRANCES: A crocodile.

REG: It's a brooch. Used to belong to my aunt.

FRANCES: It's beautiful.

> FRANCES *looks afraid to touch it.*

REG: Don't worry. It won't bite . . . You don't like it. Is that
it?

> FRANCES *looks at the crocodile for a while, touches it with
> her finger tips. There is so much going on in her mind but
> she can't find the words or – if she can – she's afraid to use
> them.*
>
> > *She looks at* REG*, then studies the crocodile once more.*

FRANCES: You hear such stories. About them. What they
do. It scares you.

REG: They're just stories. Crocodiles are harmless.

FRANCES: It scares you.

REG: They would never harm you.

> FRANCES *hands him the brooch.*

FRANCES: I want to wear it. Now. Put it on, Reg.

> REG *pins it to her dress.* FRANCES *stares at him intently.*

FRANCES (*almost a whisper*): I can see things . . .

REG: Where?

FRANCES: In your eyes.

REG: What things?

FRANCES: Monsters.

> *They kiss.*

EXT. KRAY HOUSE. DAY

Car containing REG *and* FRANCES *pulls up. There are many big, black cars parked outside the Kray house. As* REG *gets out of the car he looks at these cars.* REG *glances at* TERRY. TERRY *frowns.*

FRANCES: You sure I look alright, Reg?

REG: Oh . . . you look lovely.

FRANCES: I want to make the right impression.

REG: They'll love you. (*Points.*) That's where we live.

FRANCES (*looking at cars*): They're not all yours are they?

REG: What, luv? Oh, no. No. They're not all mine.

    They go into VIOLET's *house . . .*

INT. KRAY HOUSE, LIVING ROOM. DAY

In the living room are ROSE. MAY, HELEN, IRIS *and* VIOLET. VIOLET *is standing by window peering out.* VIOLET *goes to the table where the tea things are spread out.*

VIOLET: I'm glad I got the bone china out, Mum.

HELEN: Don't worry. Everything looks lovely. She can take
    us as she finds us.

    REG *and* FRANCES *enter the room.* FRANCES *looks
    intimidated by the sight of the women.*

REG: Mum . . . this is Frances.

    VIOLET *goes up and gives* FRANCES *a peck on the cheek.*

VIOLET: Hello, luv. Come in and make yourself at home.
    Move yourself, May.

    MAY *makes space for* FRANCES. FRANCES *sits down. All
    the women stare at her.*

HELEN: Oh, she's lovely.

MAY: An angel, Reg. Really.

ROSE: That's right. She's an angel.

MAY: An angel.

68

VIOLET: Leave her alone, you lot. (*At* REG.) Now you're here you can help me upstairs with the tea. All your mates are upstairs. You can bring the biscuits.

 VIOLET *picks up the tea-tray.* REG *glances at* FRANCES *and hesitates.* FRANCES *looks at him, lost and helpless. If she had the courage, she'd scream, 'Don't leave me here alone!'*

VIOLET: Come on, Reg.

REG (*at* FRANCES): Won't be a minute.

 REG *and* VIOLET *exit.*

IRIS (*at* FRANCES): The Twins have got a lot of friends. You'll get used to it.

INT. KRAY HOUSE, UPSTAIRS ROOM. DAY

A meeting in progress. RON, PERRY, DICKIE, GREY, WHIP, TOM *and* STRAKER. *Also there are* BILL, TIMMY, EDDIE, DENNIS, FRANK, STEVE. *They're all sitting at a long, wooden table.* RON *is at the head of the table, holding a green snake.* VIOLET *and* REG *enter.* VIOLET *puts the tea-tray on the table.*

VIOLET: There you are boys.

 General 'That's alright Mrs Kray'.

VIOLET: Now, Reg's got the biscuits. Make sure he doesn't scoff them all. (*Seeing* RON's *snake.*) Oh, really, Ron, must you have that bloody thing indoors. It's got germs, I swear it has.

RON: It's clean, Mum. Honest.

VIOLET: If you want anything else bang on the floor. I'll be downstairs with Frances. See you boys later.

ALL: Goodbye, Mrs Kray.

 VIOLET *leaves.* REG *sits at the table.*

RON (*at* REG): You're late for the meeting.

REG: I didn't know there was one.

RON: It was called urgently.

REG: By who?

RON: By me . . . Put the biscuits down.

REG *slams the biscuits on the table.*

RON (*at* REG): It's the Maltese boys.

STRAKER: It's serious, Reg. They're out of order. There were threats made at the Regal last night.

PERRY: Everyone want tea?

WHIP: No milk in mine.

DICKIE: No milk? That's disgusting.

PERRY *starts pouring the tea.*

REG: What kind of threats?

RON: There's only one kind. I told you they had to be taught a lesson. We should show them what we've got.

REG: You always think that.

RON: I'm always right.

PERRY: Biscuits?

DICKIE: Any rich tea?

PERRY: Just chocolate.

DICKIE: I'll have chocolate –

RON (*angrily*): We've let it slip, Reg, and I don't like it. The Maltese are creeping up and our eyes are elsewhere. We've got lazy. Distracted. It's got to be tightened up. These Maltese have got to go! Yeah?

ALL (*except* REG): Yeah!

INT. KRAY HOUSE, LIVING ROOM. DAY

VIOLET, MAY, HELEN *etc. as before.* HELEN *hears the rowdy 'yeahs' from upstairs and rolls her eyes.*

HELEN: Men are born children and they stay children. They scream and shout and boss people around. Like your father. They think they're in control but they don't know the half of it.

MAY (*at* FRANCES): That's a lovely outfit, pet. Really suits you.

71

FRANCES: Thank you.

HELEN: We didn't notice clothes when I was your age. When I was young –

VIOLET: More tea, Mum?

HELEN: You know what I did during the war?

ROSE: Here she goes . . .

MAY: Stop her someone . . .

VIOLET: Look, Mum, Frances doesn't want to hear all about that –

HELEN (*relentlessly*): Cut pieces of cloth for quilt making. Small pieces. No bigger than your handkerchief. And you know how many I used to cut?

ROSE/VIOLET/MAY: Four hundred . . .

HELEN: Four hundred. Four hundred an hour. Can you imagine a man doing that? Drove us mad it did. Made us want to scream. I did once too. Scream that is. Stood in the middle of the road and screamed 'til I was blue in the face. No-one batted an eyelid. Why should they? There was a lot of screaming in those days . . .
Sudden noises from above. The 'boys' start coming downstairs.

  VIOLET *opens the living room door –*

VIOLET: You making a move, boys?

TOGETHER: Yes, bye, Mrs Kray . . . Bye . . . Thank you, Mrs Kray . . .

STEVE: Lovely biscuits, Mrs Kray.

VIOLET: You're welcome, luv. Be good.

REG (*at* FRANCES): I got to go . . . Stay here. I won't be long.

FRANCES: Where you going?

REG: Business . . .

VIOLET: Oh, you boys. You'll wear yourselves out. Have you met Frances, Ron?

RON (*flatly*): Hello.

FRANCES: Hello, Ron . . .

72

RON (*tugging* REG): Come on, Reg. Car's waiting.

FRANCES: Reg, I've got to go home.

    REG *looks helpless for a second.*

VIOLET: Bye, boys.

    The helpless look vanishes, REG *pecks* VIOLET *on the cheek.*

REG: Bye, Mum.

VIOLET: Bye, my darling.

    REG *follows* RON *out of the house.*

      FRANCES *and* VIOLET *glance at each other.* VIOLET *smiles.* FRANCES *tries to smile, but fails . . .*

EXT. KRAY HOUSE. DAY

Some of the 'boys' are getting into cars. Most, however, get in the back of a big, black van, which has just pulled up. REG *and* RON *get into the van also. Van drives off, followed by the cars . . .*

INT. BACK OF VAN. DAY

It is like an armoury. Guns everywhere.

RON: Remember, lads. Scare them to fucking jelly. We want these fucking Maltese boys off the map once and for all.

    REG *stares at* RON.

      A beat.

REG: What did you think of her?

RON: Who?

REG: Frances.

RON: Very pretty.

EXT. HOSPITAL TAVERN. DAY

The 'Hospital Tavern' is a typical East End pub: on a corner, many windows with ornate, Victorian decorations.

The black van pulls up outside. RON *and* REG — *now clutching machine guns — get out. The rest of the boys follow.*

There is something smooth and effortless in the way they all move, like snakes over sand, sharks through water.

RON *and* REG *approach the pub . . .*

RON: You going to marry her?

RON *and* REG *go into the pub —*

INT. HOSPITAL TAVERN. DAY

There are five Maltese gang members at the bar. They are already tense; they've been waiting for this. One of them holds a blade. Several have knuckledusters. A BARMAID *is trembling with fear, frozen, like a rabbit in headlights.*

RON *and* REG *enter.*

REG (*to* RON): Yes.

The TWINS' *machine guns erupt into life. The five Maltese are taken by surprise. They hadn't been expecting this. What use are blades and knuckledusters against bullets.*

Bullets everywhere!

The mirror behind the bar shatters!

Glasses explode!

Wooden stools shatter!

The five Maltese dive for cover. And the bullets keep coming.

Exploding.

Shattering.

Ringing in their ears.

74

EXT. CHURCH. DAY

REG *and* FRANCES *are just leaving the church. They have just been married. Whole family around them. Throwing confetti. Church bells sound.*

INT. KRAY HOUSE, HALLWAY. NIGHT

ROSE, VIOLET *and* MAY *enter.* CHARLIE SENIOR *staggers in after them. It is after the wedding reception. Their clothes showing the signs of a long day celebrating. The women are more than a little tiddly. As for* CHARLIE SENIOR . . . *well, he's inebriated.*

VIOLET (*stiffly*): Oh, you smell awful.

CHARLIE SENIOR: Give us a kiss.

VIOLET: Go to bed, you revolting man.

 CHARLIE SENIOR *staggers upstairs.* ROSE, VIOLET *and* MAY –

INT. KRAY HOUSE, LIVING ROOM. NIGHT

– go into the living room. They throw themselves into armchairs and the sofa, exhausted.

VIOLET: Thank God there's not a wedding every day. That's all I can say.

MAY: They looked lovely, though, didn't they?

VIOLET: They did, didn't they, May. My own son married. And on his honeymoon. You know I still can't believe it. Do you think I've lost him, May?

MAY: Reg? You must be joking. You'll always be first, you know that.

 ROSE *is just staring, lost in a world of her own. A melancholy world, which is unlike her.*

VIOLET: What's the matter, Rose?

No response.

VIOLET: Rose?

ROSE: I was just thinking . . . You know, I was on the bus the other day and some old toe-rag was boasting about all he'd suffered in the war . . . Stupid old . . . I tell you, they don't know. It was the women who had the war. The real war. The women were left at home in the shit, not sitting in some sparkling plane or gleaming tank. There was no glamour for us. They should have been with me when old Pauline Wooley went into labour. Remember that, Violet?

VIOLET: Yes, yes, I do, darling.

ROSE: Seven hours of screaming down Bethnal Green bloody tube station. And then I had to cut the baby's head off to save the mother's life. She died anyway, poor old cow. God, there was so much blood . . . Jesus. And the abortions . . . Those poor girls . . . One day they'll drain Victoria Park lake, and you know what they'll find? What glorious remnants of the Second World War? Babies! That's what. Bullets and dead babies. Men! Mum's right. They stay kids all their fucking lives and they end up heroes. Or monsters. Either way they win. Women have to grow up. If they stay children, they become victims . . .

ROSE *begins to cough violently. She appears to be in some convulsion.* VIOLET *and the others rush to her.*

VIOLET: Rose? What is it? Oh, May . . .

ROSE *coughs some blood . . .*

INT. ROSE'S HOUSE, BEDROOM. NIGHT

ROSE *is lying in bed.* RON *sits beside her, holding her hand.* VIOLET, HELEN *and* MAY *are in the room.*

ROSE *is in the middle of a convulsion. It's very violent. The family watches on, helpless.*

76

ROSE *clutches* RON's *hand tighter. She stares into his eyes, unable to talk.* RON *stares back, willing her to live. But – There's nothing anyone can do.*

Suddenly, ROSE's *body relaxes. She slumps back in the bed, dead.*

RON *starts to cry. His tears are uncontrollable. He grabs at the sheets, pulls at them.* RON *is out of his mind with grief. He grabs hold of* VIOLET.

RON: Get Reggie back! Stop his honeymoon! Stop his honeymoon!

　　RON *runs out of the room . . .*
VIOLET: Ron! Ron!

EXT. ROSE'S HOUSE. NIGHT
RON *runs out of* ROSE's *house.* RON *starts to kick at the dustbins. Knocks them over.*

Neighbours come out.

RON *kicks over more dustbins, pushes at a brick wall. He is howling with grief, howling like a wild animal. He falls to his knees and shrieks at the night sky –*

RON: REGGIE!!!

EXT. CLIFFS BY SEA. DAY
FRANCES *and* REG *are having a picnic.*

It is a bright, idyllic (if windy) sunny day. The kind of day you only get when you are very much in love.

REG *is winding some film into his camera.* FRANCES *is holding him, resting her chin on his shoulder.*

FRANCES: It's funny . . . I don't miss anyone. Do you, Reg? Miss anyone?
REG: No. No-one.

77

FRANCES *kisses his neck and cheek.*

FRANCES: Everything about you is different here. You know that?

REG: How?

FRANCES: I don't know. I can't explain. Your skin feels different, your body feels different . . . You even smell different.

REG: Well, you look the same. Just as beautiful.

They kiss.

REG: I want a photograph of us. Together like this . . .

REG *balances the camera on a nearby rock, frames it on* FRANCES, *then sets the timer.* REG *positions himself next to* FRANCES.

We become the viewpoint of the camera. We see REG *and* FRANCES *stare into the camera at us. We hear the whirling and clicking of the timer inside the camera. Then . . .*

Click!

The shutter shuts to black . . .

Once the photograph is taken (and we are no longer POV of camera), FRANCES *gives* REG *a hug. As she does so, she looks over his shoulder . . .*

A black Daimler is pulling up. WHIP *is driving. The car parks at a slight distance.* WHIP *gets out . . . but does not come over. He remains by the car.*

FRANCES (*softly*): Reg?

REG *looks, sees* WHIP. WHIP *motions for* REG *to come over.*

REG: I don't bloody believe it! (*Pecks* FRANCES *on cheek.*) Wait there a sec.

REG *gets up and, leaving* FRANCES, *goes to* WHIP. WHIP *whispers something in* REG's *ear.* REG *listens, then falls into* WHIP's *arms.* WHIP *embraces him, then helps him into the car.* REG's *face is buried in his hands.*

FRANCES *stares on — worried, confused.*

INT. RON'S FLAT, BEDROOM. DAY

Slowly, the camera pans round to reveal a chandelier, satin cushions, velvet wallpaper, brass candelabra . . .

Two people are naked in the bed. One of them is RON. *We can't make out the other person yet.*

The phone starts ringing. RON *reaches out and answers it.*

RON: Yeah . . . He's *what*? Keep him there! I want to talk to him myself.

Now we see —

The figure next to him is STEVE. *He sits up, rubs his eyes.* RON *slams the phone down angrily, gets up, starts to dress.*

STEVE: What was that all about?

RON: Bloody Jack the Hat. He gets on my tits. Got to go.

STEVE: Do you want me to come with you?

RON: No. Get out and talk to people. Give them that charming smile of yours. I'm fed up with all this crap with Jack. He's a pain in the bloody neck.

STEVE: Well, don't take it out on me. It ain't my fault.

RON *throws* STEVE*'s clothes from the end of the bed.*

RON: Look at all your bloody crap here. Shoes everywhere. Pants in the bath. Just clean up after yourself. Everything's getting too damn messy.

INT. DOUBLE R CLUB, OFFICE. DAY

REG *is sitting behind a very long desk. In front of him stands a frail, nervous looking man. He's about fifty years old, but looks older. Despite his frailty, nerves and age, there's a spiteful streak to him. An instinctive viciousness — that warns you to keep a distance. In short, he's not to be trusted. His name is* JACK THE HAT.

GREY, DICKIE *and* TERRY *are scattered round the room, watching.*

REG: Just be grateful it's me you're dealing with and not
    Ron. He'd have your guts for garters, Jack, you know
    that.

JACK: It was a mistake, Reg, really –

REG: You ripped us off, Jack!

JACK: It was a mistake. Really. A mistake. I wouldn't do it.
    Reg, you know I wouldn't do it. Grey, Dickie . . . you
    know me –

GREY: Oh, I know you alright.

JACK: I just wouldn't do it.

REG (*at* JACK): Wait outside.

JACK: But I –

REG: Just do it!

    JACK *goes out*.

GREY: He's been good in the past.

REG: We'll watch him. He's scared. He knows we know.

INT. DOUBLE R CLUB, CORRIDOR AND STAIRS. DAY
REG *and* GREY *leave the office. Outside* JACK *is waiting.* REG
walks down the corridor and down the stairs. JACK *trails
behind them.*

REG: You stay, but we're watching. You're already one foot
    in the grave, Jack, don't jump in head first, there's a
    good boy.

    REG *pats* JACK*'s cheek*.

JACK (*almost whispering*): Reg . . . I wouldn't do anything to
    . . . pals, Reg. Pals.

REG: I hope so, Jack.

    REG *leaves*. JACK *follows like a puppy* . . .

EXT. DOUBLE R CLUB. DAY
A car pulls up. RON *jumps out.* REG *comes out of the club and
motions him to stay in the car.*

81

REG: It's dealt with.

RON: I want to . . .

REG (*firmer*): It's dealt with!

> RON *is glaring at* JACK THE HAT, *who stands in the doorway.* GREY *stands next to* JACK.

RON (*angrily*): You're in trouble, Jack!

> REG *gets in the car, then* RON.

RON: You should have done him, Reg. He's trouble.

REG: I've done all we had to. He's afraid. He ain't going to rip us off again.

RON: We should have done him. Remember I said that.

> *The car drives off.*

JACK: Stupid bastards!

GREY: You're not fooling anyone, Jack. Those bloody tablets of yours. They're turning your mind to jelly. All they're going to do is dig you an early grave.

JACK: They're a couple of bloody kids.

GREY: I'd park those lips of yours if I was you, Jack. They're going to get you in big trouble.

JACK: Who from? I'm not afraid of the Krays. Pair of fucking freaks.

INT. KRAY HOUSE, UPSTAIRS ROOM. DAY

REG *and* RON *and their brother,* CHARLIE JUNIOR, *are talking to* SAM RIPLEY *and* CHRIS RIPLEY. *Two brothers in their early thirties. They are dressed in suits and ties. Also in the room is* DICKIE.

> *It's quite clear from what the Ripley Brothers are wearing, and their demeanour, that they are in the same 'business' as the Krays.*

> *This is not a social call.*

REG: We can live together. The Ripley Brothers. The Kray Brothers. We ain't got any argument.

SAM: That's true. We've never trod on each other's toes. But there are others . . .

REG (*hissing*): The Pellam Brothers. And Cornell.

RON: I wouldn't worry about Cornell.

SAM: Their torturer.

CHARLIE JUNIOR: Their what?

SAM: Listen. I've seen what he can do. So has Chris. He can do no end of things with a pair of pliers.

CHARLIE JUNIOR: That's disgusting.

REG: How much influence is Cornell with the Pellams?

SAM: Well, he's an influence. And he's got it in for you boys. You know that.

RON: It's just a personal thing really. Between me and Cornell. He's been calling me names.

SAM: Why does he hate you so much?

RON: Bad chemistry.

INT. KRAY HOUSE, KITCHEN. DAY

VIOLET *is making a pot of tea for the boys upstairs. She's almost totally grey now: but still a strong-looking woman.*

FRANCES *is sitting, fiddling with her gloves. She no longer has the vitality she had earlier. She's not so much fragile as broken and held together by haute couture. She's fiddling with her gloves as if she still hasn't worked out what they're for.*

VIOLET: I lose track. Really I do. How many clubs they got now? Three? Young Charlie took me to the Regal the other night . . . You can take those gloves off now, darling. You'll stain them.

FRANCES: Reg likes them. They go with the outfit.

VIOLET: I'm sure he does. But Reg's not here now is he, so take them off, there's a good girl.

The two women look at each other.

A beat.

FRANCES *starts removing the gloves* . . .

VIOLET: Well, I better get this tea up to those young men.
They must be gasping. Haven't stopped nattering since
they went up there.

VIOLET *leaves with the tea-tray* . . .

INT. KRAY HOUSE, UPSTAIRS ROOM. DAY
As before, the TWINS *and Ripley brothers etc.*

REG: . . . We're expecting visitors from across the ocean.
Soon you ain't going to be able to throw a brick without
hitting someone that belongs to us. It's getting too big
to let the likes of Cornell get in our way. He's a maggot.
And we're big fish. Big fish who own the ocean.

VIOLET (*from outside*): Someone open the door please.

DICKIE *opens the door.* VIOLET *enters with the tea-tray
and puts it on the table. The men all say 'hello'.* VIOLET
smiles back, pleased to see them.

VIOLET: Now I don't want to be a nuisance, but someone's
trod in something.

The men look at each other, fazed.

VIOLET: I don't mind who it is. Accidents will happen. But
do you mind checking?

A slight pause. Then . . . RON *checks the sole of his shoe.
Then they all check.*

VIOLET: Anyone?

RON: No. Not me, Mum.

REG: Nor me, Mum.

VIOLET: No! Dickie?

DICKIE: No, Mrs Kray.

VIOLET: Boys?

SAM RIPLEY: No, Mrs Kray.

CHRIS RIPLEY: No, Mrs Kray.

VIOLET: Oh, well, perhaps it's Frances. How's your mother, Dickie?

DICKIE: Oh, she's fine thanks, Mrs Kray.

VIOLET: Give her my love, won't you?

DICKIE: Yes. Thanks.

VIOLET: Just knock on the floor if you want something.

VIOLET *exits . . .*

INT. KRAY HOUSE, PARLOUR. DAY

FRANCES *is staring into space, the gloves in her lap.* VIOLET *enters, still confused about the mess up the stairs.*

VIOLET: Frances, I don't want to be a pest but . . . (*Notices* FRANCES' *blank expression.*) Frances?

FRANCES: Oh . . . Sorry. What?

A beat.

VIOLET *kneels down beside her.*

VIOLET: Look luv, I'm going to ask you something. And if you think I'm being an interfering old cow, then just tell me to mind my own business and I'll shut up. But . . . you're not still taking those . . . tablets are you?

FRANCES (*aghast*): Who told you about them?

VIOLET: Well, Reg, of course.

FRANCES: Well he had no right to tell you.

VIOLET: I'm his mother. Reggie tells me everything.

FRANCES: . . . No! I'm not taking any tablets.

VIOLET: Is it Reg?

FRANCES: No . . . Oh, I don't know. Yes, it's Reg. It's me. It's everything. I don't know. It's just that . . . I feel I'm being taken over. I haven't got any strength. I don't know who I am.

VIOLET: That's just called being married, darling.

FRANCES: I don't believe that. Sometimes I wake up and I think, How old am I? What music do I like? What films

85

do I like? And I don't know the answer anymore. All I know is what Reg likes me to like. What Reg likes me to like. Like . . . like these bloody gloves . . .

FRANCES *throws the gloves to the floor. She rushes out of the kitchen . . .*

   VIOLET *picks up the gloves and stares at them thoughtfully.*

INT. KRAY HOUSE, HALLWAY/STAIRS. DAY
FRANCES *rushes upstairs and into bedroom. She is crying.*

INT. KRAY HOUSE, UPSTAIRS ROOM. DAY
Everyone is dunking biscuits into tea.

DICKIE: Everyone's talking to me lately. Never knew I had so many friends. I think they find me a bit glamorous.
RON: That's exactly right. And you know what glamour is?
DICKIE: No.
RON: It's fear. I learnt that ages ago. If people are afraid of you, you can do anything. The glamour is fear.
   There's a knock at the door and VIOLET *pokes her head in.*
VIOLET: Only me, boys. I'm being a pest, I know.
   General 'Not at all, Mrs Kray'.
RON: What is it, Mum?
VIOLET (*at* REG): Reg, can I have a word please, darling.
   REG *goes to* VIOLET.
REG: What's wrong, Mum?
   VIOLET *motions him outside.*

INT. KRAY HOUSE, BEDROOM. DAY
FRANCES *is sitting on a bed, weeping.* REG *enters.*
86

REG (*softly*): Frances.

FRANCES: Oh, hello, Reg. Is your meeting over?

REG: Yes.

FRANCES: Oh . . . good.

> REG, *slowly, makes his way to* FRANCES. *He sits beside her on the bed.*

REG: What's wrong, luv?

FRANCES: Wrong? Nothing.

REG: But Mum said –

FRANCES: Oh, goodness. Can't I say or do anything here without everyone telling everyone.

REG: What's wrong? Tell me! I want to help.

FRANCES: I don't . . . I can't . . . Oh, Reg! I don't know what's wrong. Really.

REG: But . . . is it me?

FRANCES: No, Reg.

REG: Don't you love me?

FRANCES: Oh, Reg. I do. I do.

> REG *is getting upset now.*

REG: Because I love you, Frances. I love you so much. I don't know what to do. Oh, Frances, what can I do? You name it.

FRANCES: Don't upset yourself, Reg.

REG: But how can I not be upset? To see you like this. How can I not be?

> REG *buries his face in his hands.*

FRANCES: Oh, Reg. Don't. It's nothing. It's just me. Me being silly. Don't be upset, Reg. Don't.

REG: I can't bear to see you like this.

FRANCES: Like what? Look at me. I'm fine. (*Puts her arms round* REG.) Everything will be fine, Reg. I love you, Reg. I love you, Reg. I love you. I love you. I love you.

EXT. KRAY HOUSE. DAY

REG *and* FRANCES *are saying goodbye to* VIOLET *and* RON.
FRANCES *still looks a little tearful. She gets straight into the
waiting car, almost trance-like.* REG *kisses* VIOLET *goodbye.*

REG: See you, Mum.

VIOLET: Bye.

> REG *gets in the car. It drives away.* RON *and* VIOLET
> *stand on the doorstep, looking after the car.* FRANCES'
> *state obviously bothers* VIOLET.

RON: She looks really beautiful.

VIOLET: Yes, she does.

RON: What's wrong with her?

> *A beat.*

VIOLET: I don't think it's possible to love someone too
much. But I think you can love them in the wrong way
. . . Oh, I don't know. (*Sighs.*) Love.

RON: She's well looked after.

VIOLET: I know, I know. She's just got to start kicking,
that's all. Like I had to. I know Reggie's my son and –
God knows – I love him . . . But she's just got to start
kicking.

EXT. EAST END PUB. NIGHT

Establishing shot of a pub.

> *Light from its windows reflect on the wet pavement. Laughter
and music from inside.*

INT. EAST END PUB. NIGHT

*The pub is crowded; a cheerful, playfully disordered Saturday
night. Air thick with smoke.*

> STEVE *is standing at the bar with a few friends. He is flushed
with alcohol and laughter – someone's just cracked a joke, and it
must have been a good one. Their laughter is cut short by –*

CORNELL: Well, well, well. All the pretty boys together.

> CORNELL *is in his late fifties, well built, and as gleefully vicious as they come. If there was a vacancy for Public Executioner he'd be there like a shot. He's not happy unless he's causing trouble. That's why he's grinning now –*

STEVE: Piss off, Cornell.

CORNELL: How's your boyfriend lately? Still in tears over his auntie?

STEVE: You want to watch your mouth.

CORNELL: What's that?

STEVE: I'm warning you, Corn –

> CORNELL *grabs him by the shirt collar.*

CORNELL: Poofs don't warn anyone! You listening? You tell that fat poof of yours he doesn't scare me. D'you hear? I hear there's yanky friends from America coming over. You tell him he's getting ideas above his station. He can own all he likes but his mother's apron strings are the handcuffs he was born with. Night, girls.

> CORNELL *strides away. The crowd parts in front of him as instinctively as fish before a shark.* STEVE *and his friends are visibly shaken.*

FRIEND: You going to tell Ron?

STEVE: Don't think I have to. Half the fucking pub heard him.

EXT. STREET WITH NEWSAGENTS. DAY

REG *and* FRANCES *driving up in a car. It parks outside a paper shop.*

> *It is early Sunday morning, the streets relatively empty. Distant sound of church bells.*

> REG *gets out, then looks back through the window at* FRANCES.

REG: Do you want some sweets?

90

FRANCES: No thank you.

REG: They'll do you good. You're losing a bit of weight. I'll get you some.

FRANCES is a mere shell now, her desire to fight back all but gone. If REG wants her to have sweets, then she'll have sweets. No point in arguing: she'd never win.

FRANCES: Alright.

INT. NEWSAGENTS. DAY

NEWSAGENT *serving. A few people are queuing.*

NEWSAGENT (*to customer*): . . . and with your cigarettes, that's thirteen and seven.

REG *enters.*

NEWSAGENT: How's it going, Reg?

REG: Mustn't grumble. Yourself?

NEWSAGENT *ignores the other customers and serves REG first.*

NEWSAGENT: 'Bout the same. How's your Mum?

REG: Oh, she is fine. You know Mum . . .

As the NEWSAGENT speaks, REG – through the shop window – sees two men talking to FRANCES as she sits in the car.

NEWSAGENT: I saw your Aunt May. She's looking alright.

REG: I'll tell her you said so.

REG *picks up a bag of sweets and goes to pay –*

NEWSAGENT: Oh, no, no. That's fine.

REG: Thanks.

NEWSAGENT: Any time, Reg. Any time.

REG *leaves the newsagents and –*

EXT. STREET WITH NEWSAGENTS. DAY

– walks up to the two men by the car.

REG (*angrily*): What's going on?

FIRST MAN: Just looking at the car, mate.

REG: What about it?

FIRST MAN: I was admiring.

SECOND MAN: Don't see many of these about.

REG: You lying bastards! You're not interested in the car!
You're interested in what's in it –

REG *hits the two men and a fight starts.*

We see the fight from inside the car with FRANCES . . .
Faces pressed flat against the window-screen.
The metal of the car reverberating with the thuds . . .
There's blood on the windscreen . . .
Still REG *punches and kicks . . .*
FRANCES *is screaming . . .*

FRANCES *panics. She goes to get out just as a man falls
back against the car door. It slams shut again.*
Punch!
Blood!
Kick!
Scream!

FRANCES: Reggie! No! No! Please! No!
Punch!
Blood!
Kick!
Scream!
*Finally, in desperation, she turns the radio on as loud as
she can. It helps to cut out the noise. She is petrified.*

INT. THE REGAL, MAIN ROOM. NIGHT

*The room is decorated with red velvet, gold brocade, chandelier,
candles, huge rosewood table. In a word, palatial.*

RON *and* REG *are the kings. Sitting at the head of the table,
holding court. Around them are* PERRY, WHIP, TIMMY,
DENNIS, *very stiff and formal, like palace guards.*

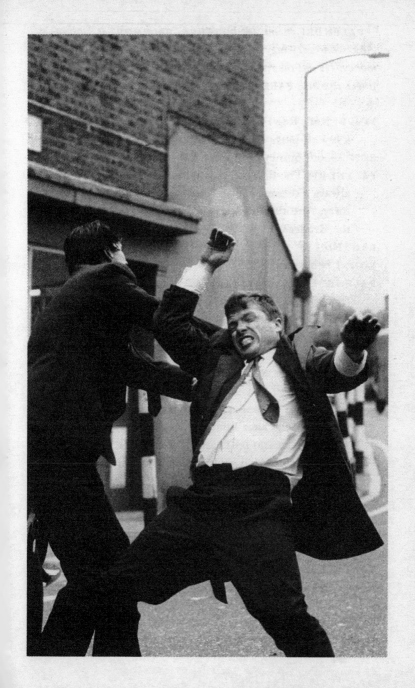

PALENDRI *enters, led by* STEVE. PALENDRI *is Italian-American: very big, very smart, reeking of money, dangerous money. He has the relaxed air of a man who knows a flick of his finger can kill.* PALENDRI *is surrounded by four bodyguards.*

STEVE: Ron, Reg . . . Mr Palendri.
> *They all shake hands and take seats.*

RON: Good journey, Mr Palendri?

PALENDRI: The flight was a nightmare. But England is always a dream. I love London. It's so wonderfully dirty. And the Beatles. I adore the Beatles. You know the Beatles?

REG: No.

RON: I believe they know us.

PALENDRI: I'm sure they do. We know of you. The ocean can be a puddle in our business. News travels fast. (*Something crosses his mind.*) Oh, how does that song go now? My wife sings it all the time. 'Can't Buy Me Love'. Great song. 'Money Can't Buy Me Love'. Trouble is, it can. Money can buy you anything. Anything you like. It can buy love, respect, loyalty, anything. It's wonderful being alive.

RON: The options have limited appeal.
> PALENDRI *snaps his fingers. A bodyguard opens a briefcase. Inside is a golden, double-headed snake. It is decorated with jewels.*

PALENDRI: For you . . . We've heard of your admiration for our reptilian brothers.
> *Bodyguard places it on table in front of* RON *and* REG. RON *picks up the snake.*

RON: It's beautiful.

PALENDRI: A mere bauble.
> REG *has taken a framed photograph from the desk drawer. It is of* RON *and* REG *with* VIOLET, MAY, ROSE *and* HELEN. *He hands it to* PALENDRI.

94

REG: And this is for you. It's us . . . with our Mum . . .
    and –
RON: – that's our Aunt Rose . . . our grandmother –
REG: – and our Aunt May.
PALENDRI: Yes . . . yes . . . Are you all Cock-en-neys?
RON/REG: Yes.
PALENDRI: You've done very well. And this is only the
    beginning. Your family and my family . . . we shall do
    lots and lots of business together.
    STEVE *has been pouring glasses of champagne. Everyone
    takes one.*
REG (*raising his glass*): To family.
PALENDRI: To family!
    They clink glasses . . .

EXT. JUNKYARD. DAY
*The junkyard mainly consists of old cars. If there can be such a
thing as a high quality junkyard, then this is it. A burning
brazier. Stray dogs.*
    CORNELL *walks through the yard, clutching a newspaper.
    Up some wooden steps . . . Towards the office . . .*

INT. OFFICE IN JUNKYARD. DAY
CHARLIE PELLAM *is sitting at a desk.* EDDIE, *his brother, is
standing by a window. Both brothers are in their mid-forties
and dressed in very expensive suits. Again, just one look tells
you 'gangster'.*
    *The office looks extremely plush, considering the surround-
ings. A smart secretary,* MISS LETT, *is taking notes.*

EDDIE: Cornell's coming.
CHARLIE: What does he want? I thought he wasn't
    supposed to leave his coffin when the sun was out.

CORNELL *enters. He looks tense, angry, wanting an argument.*

CORNELL: Those Kray brothers are getting on my tits.

CHARLIE (*at* MISS LETT): That'll be all Miss Lett.

MISS LETT: Sir?

CHARLIE *indicates she should go.* MISS LETT *gets up and squeezes by* CORNELL.

MISS LETT (*flatly*): Excuse me.

MISS LETT *exits.*

CHARLIE: You know, Cornell, it's amazing you can walk at all with your foot in your mouth so much.

CORNELL *angrily slams the newspaper on the desk. There's a photograph of the* TWINS *donating money to charity. The headline reads: 'BUSINESS MEN AID CHARITY BOXING NIGHT'.*

CORNELL: You seen this?

EDDIE: Surprise us. What is it?

CORNELL: Kray brothers. Splattered all over the bloody paper. Bloody heroes they are. This to charity. That to charity. The other to charity.

CHARLIE (*coolly*): What does it matter?

CORNELL (*angrily*): What does it matter? I'm out there. Earwigging on the street. And what I'm hearing is, 'Kray, Kray, Kray, Kray, Kray!' The pavement stinks with Krays.

EDDIE: Cornell, we've been through this a million times. The Krays are not interested in us. Course they will be if you don't shut that megaphone of a voice box.

CORNELL: You don't know! You don't know what they're saying about you. They're saying things.

CHARLIE: Things! What things?

CORNELL: Things! I say, 'Shoot the bastards!' What are they? A pair of bum boys. Let's put them out of their misery. A pair of movie gangsters. All they're interested in is what they look like. They make me sick! They're a

96

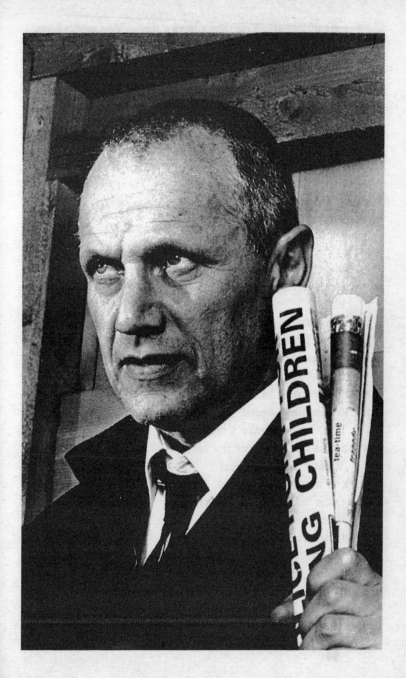

pair of locusts. You won't have a thing. You won't have the pants you're sitting in, unless we do something now. They walk round the streets like kings. King ponses! And you know why? They own the fucking street. So what I say is, 'Bang! Bang!' All over. Nice and sweet. End of agro.

EXT. STREET. DAY

JACK THE HAT *driving down the street. He is flustered and angry. His girlfriend is eating from a bag of sweets. She is overweight.*

JACK: . . . bloody shit on their shoes. Jack do this, Jack do that. Well, I won't stand for it, you hear. It's not right. I'm older than them. I know things. Bloody fucking kids.

GIRLFRIEND (*offers bag of sweets*): Do you want one?

JACK: No I don't fucking want one. Stuff your sweets! Always eating you are. Like a fucking dustbin. Why don't you give 'em a rest.

GIRLFRIEND: I like sweets.

JACK: You like sweets! You're getting fat. You know that? I don't want to take a fat cow out like you.

GIRLFRIEND: Oh, give it a rest, Jack. I'm fat, you're bald. What's the difference!

JACK: I'm not bloody bald. I told you. I am not bald!
JACK *starts pushing her savagely. Girlfriend screams, the door opens behind her. She shrieks.*

GIRLFRIEND: For God's sake, Jack. Stop it. Stop . . .
Suddenly JACK *kicks her out. Girlfriend falls to the ground with a sickening thump.*

INT. MAY'S HOUSE, LIVING ROOM. DAY

MAY *is facing* RON *and* REG.

MAY: Her mother depends on her, Ron. She's a cripple
herself. You would think someone would do something.
I mean, this man they say did it . . . this Jack somebody
. . . I mean, you would think he was employed by
somebody. And you would think this somebody would
feel responsible for what has happened . . . help in some
way, eh? (*Glares at the* TWINS.) . . . Well, wouldn't
you?

REG: Yes. You would, Aunt May.

RON: Yes. They should make sure they're alright. The girl
and her mother.

MAY: Well, yes. Exactly what I was thinking. The least they
should do. You know, make sure they're not short of
money, pay their rent.

RON: Of course.

MAY: Of course.

AUNT MAY *smiles.*

INT. REGGIE'S HOUSE, BEDROOM. DAY
The room is full of new clothes.
  Dresses hang everywhere . . .
  New shoes cover the floor . . .
  Coats over the bed . . .
  FRANCES *stands in the middle of the room, looking*
bewildered. REG *is admiring the dresses*

REG: You like them?

FRANCES: But wh . . . what does it mean, Reg? I don't
understand.

REG: They're all for you. Every one. One for every night of
the year.

  FRANCES *is lost.*

FRANCES: But Reg –

REG: You don't like them.

99

FRANCES: It's not that –

REG: You do like them? *I* like them.

FRANCES: That's just it. *You* like them. You can't dress me like this Reg. I've always bought my own clothes.

REG: But you don't have to anymore.

FRANCES: Have to? What do you mean, have to? It's not a case of having to. I want to.

REG: But you can't afford it. And I can. I love giving you things. You are my bloody wife. I have to look after you. Anyway . . . it's not as if you've got any money of your own, is it?

FRANCES (*flatly*): That's right. I've got no money.

REG: So I get them.

FRANCES *stares.* REG *picks up a dress.*

REG: This one is really for you, Fran. Don't you think? You wear it tonight. You'll be the prettiest thing there.

REG *kisses her forehead.*

INT. WEST END CLUB. NIGHT
In a word; plush.
  Clinking glasses . . .
  A celebrity singing . . .
  Audience watching . . .
  In the audience are REG *and* FRANCES, CHARLIE *and*
IRIS, RON *and* STEVE. *They watch, enraptured, as the singer,*
JUDY, *sings. When she is finished she comes over to the boys.*

RON: That was lovely, Judy.

JUDY: Thank you, Ron.

REG: You're in good voice tonight, Judy.

JUDY: Well, I croaked in time. (*Looking at* FRANCES.) You alright? Looks like you need a drink.

REG: She's fine. This is my brother's wife, Iris.

IRIS: You look terrific.

100

JUDY: So do you. Now, you boys . . . how are you?

RON/REG: Fine, Judy –

> *They are interrupted as the paparazzi rush over.*

JUDY (*sitting with the boys*): Oh, well, boys, duty calls.

> *Everyone loves the attention.*
> *They really lap it up.*
> *Everyone, that is, except* FRANCES.
> *She flinches as every flashlight goes off.*
>> *Flash! Flash!*

PAPARAZZI: Look this way, Ron.

> *Flash! Flash!*

RON: Sure. Like this?

PAPARAZZI: That's it . . . Reg, move closer to your brother.

> *Flash! Flash!*

REG: Sure.

> *Flash!*

PAPARAZZI: This way, Reg . . . This way, Ron . . . Frances, move in.

> *Flash!*

FRANCES: . . . Sorry?

> *Flash!*
>> *Flash!*

PAPARAZZI: Frances! Frances! Frances!

FRANCES: . . . What?

> *Flash!*
>> *Flash!*
>> *Flash-flinch!*
>> *Flash-flinch!*
>> *Flash-flinch!*

INT. WEST END CLUB, POWDER ROOM. NIGHT

FRANCES *is re-touching her make-up. She looks a little shaken.*

> IRIS *enters.*

101

IRIS: You alright, luv?

FRANCES: Oh, yes.

IRIS: You look a little peaky. Not eaten anything have you?

FRANCES: No.

IRIS: Drunk too much. The boys don't like it if we drink too much, you know.

FRANCES: No.

IRIS *starts to re-touch her make-up.* FRANCES *takes a deep breath before –*

FRANCES: Iris. . . ?

IRIS: Yes, luv?

FRANCES: How do you stand it?

IRIS: What, luv?

FRANCES: Everything. How do you cope?

IRIS *looks at* FRANCES *deep and hard.*

IRIS: Listen, luv. You just carry on. That's all you do. You carry on. You shop. You buy things. You smile. Look good. And you don't say a word. You keep saying, 'Everything is perfect and I'm happy.' You say it two hundred times a day. Until . . . you believe it. Everything is perfect. You are happy. And then you re-touch your lippy.

FRANCES: But what . . . what if I can't?

IRIS: There is no can't.

FRANCES: I remember reading this story once. About a woman. She was walking her baby across some cliff tops. The baby was in a pram. Everything's beautiful. Sunshine. Everything. And then, suddenly, out of nowhere . . . a thunderstorm. Lightning. The mother runs . . . But then, she's struck. Struck by lightning. It doesn't kill her. But it paralyses her. She can't move. Falls to the ground. And the pram . . . Oh, the pram! It goes rolling away from her. She's laying there and the pram goes rolling towards the edge of the cliff. The mother can't do anything about it. She just watches. As

102

the pram goes over the ledge. She can't move. Can't even scream.

IRIS *stares at* FRANCES *for a long beat. Then she takes* FRANCES' *lipstick from* FRANCES' *hand and re-touches* FRANCES' *make-up.*

FRANCES *stares at her.*

IRIS: There! You look perfect now.

FRANCES (*softly*): Thank you.

IRIS: Anything to help, luv.

INT. WEST END CLUB, LOBBY. NIGHT

REG *and* CHARLIE *are helping* FRANCES *and* IRIS *on with their coats.* RON *is watching.* STEVE *is standing by the main door of the lobby. As they approach doors* CHARLIE PELLAM *(and his wife* SALLY*) and* EDDIE PELLAM *(and his wife* SHARON*) enter.* CORNELL *is with them.*

SHARON *is wearing the same dress as* FRANCES. *They seem to know each other and laugh and joke about it.* FRANCES' *earlier anxiety immediately disappears.*

REG: You've missed the show.

CHARLIE PELLAM: We've come to eat.

RON *and* CORNELL *stare at each other.*

EDDIE: You know Cornell, don't you?

RON: We've heard about him.

CORNELL (*at* RON): Alright?

RON: Alright.

EDDIE: He's a great fan.

SHARON *and* FRANCES *are still laughing about the dresses . . .*

SHARON (*laughing*): . . . Just as well you're going, luv. Isn't it embarrassing! It's just the thing you always dread.

FRANCES: You fill it better than me, Shar.

SHARON: It's called getting fat, luv. So how are you?

103

REG *tugs at* FRANCES *to stop her talking.* EDDIE *does the same to* SHARON.

  EDDIE *and* REG *are glaring at each other.*

EDDIE: I let my wife buy her own dress for tonight. That's why there's this lapse in taste.

REG (*angrily*): Yeah?

  REG *steps forward, going for* EDDIE. CHARLIE *holds him back.* EDDIE *looks at* RON, *then* STEVE.

CORNELL (*at* RON): When are you two getting married?

  RON *steps forward, going for* EDDIE.

RON: Yeah? Yeah?

  REG *holds him back. The atmosphere is close to spontaneous combustion.*

REG: Leave it, Ron . . . Leave it.

  The Pellams and their wives go into the main club.

SHARON (*over her shoulder*): Bye, Fran.

FRANCES: Yeah. Bye, luv.

RON: I'm going to get Cornell –

REG: I said leave it. He's not worth it. You hear me?

RON: Piece of shit!

  RON, STEVE, CHARLIE, IRIS *make their way up stairs to the front door.* REG *takes* FRANCES *to one side.*

REG: I didn't know you knew Charlie Pellam's wife.

FRANCES: We went to school together.

REG: Well, stay away.

FRANCES: But Reg! She's my friend!

REG: Not anymore she's not.

FRANCES: But –

REG: Just do it, luv! For me! No argument! There's a good girl.

  REG *moves away.*

  FRANCES *remains motionless. She is trembling, staring after* REG.

  Lifelessly, she follows the others towards –

INT. WEST END CLUB, STAIRS. NIGHT
– *the bottom step. There are mirrors all round. She is standing on a prism of her own image.*

Suddenly, from the very centre of her, a scream breaks free. It is both terrifying and heartbreaking. A piercing shriek from the soul that threatens to shatter the glass all round her.

INT. GROCERY SHOP. DAY
Shopkeeper is serving. There are about six customers waiting to be served. One of whom has a six-year-old girl with her.

FRANCES *comes in. Shopkeeper immediately ignores the other woman and turns his attention to* FRANCES.

SHOPKEEPER: And what can I do for you today –
FIRST CUSTOMER: Hang on a moment. I've been here for –
SHOPKEEPER: – Mrs Kray!
> *This shuts* FIRST CUSTOMER *up.*
FRANCES: Oh, well . . . (*Takes list from purse.*) . . . I've got this.
> FRANCES *hands a list to shopkeeper. Shopkeeper starts to get the things together.*
SHOPKEEPER: And how's Reg?
FRANCES: Oh . . . fine.
SHOPKEEPER: And Ron?
FRANCES: Yes, fine.
> *Gradually,* FRANCES *becomes aware that the customers in the shop are staring at her.* FRANCES *looks away, trying to quell the rising panic. She fumbles in her purse.*
SHOPKEEPER: And your mother? How's she?
FRANCES: My . . . my mother!
SHOPKEEPER: Violet.
FRANCES: Oh, yes, my mother . . .

105

FRANCES *looks over at the girl. The girl stares at*
FRANCES. *The panic rises in* FRANCES *even more. She*
drops some coins. They roll under the counter.

FRANCES: I . . . I'm sorry . . . I . . .

   Shopkeeper puts a carrier bag full of FRANCES' *shopping*
   in front of her.

SHOPKEEPER: There we are. And I've slipped some of
   Reg's favourite salmon in. He does like red, eh?

   The whole thing is a nightmare now. There is something
   horrifically grotesque about the shopkeeper. Something
   menacing about the staring women.

   And that child . . . staring . . .

   Staring . . .

FRANCES (*faintly, glancing at child*): How much . . . do –
   Staring!

   Staring!

SHOPKEEPER: Oh, don't worry about that. You just tell
   Reg I said hello.

   FRANCES' *rising panic bubbles over now. She can't take it*
   anymore. She runs from the shop and –

EXT. STREET. DAY

– *scarpers down the street with shopping.*
   She is almost hysterical.
   She drops the shopping.
   Runs faster . . .
   Faster . . .
   Faster . . .

INT. REGGIE'S HOUSE, BEDROOM. DAY

FRANCES' *face is blank, expressionless. She is sitting at the*
dressing table removing her make-up and combing out her hair.
Then, slowly, she removes her jewellery. Then strips to her slip.

She walks over to the bed. Sits on the edge of the
mattress.
She takes a bottle of tablets from the bedside cabinet. She
takes a handful, then another. She can't swallow them quick
enough.
She gags on them . . . but still swallows.
More tablets.
Swallowing . . .
Swallowing . . .
Lays down on the bed. Reaches out for a photograph on the
bedside cabinet. It is the one that was taken on their honeymoon,
on the cliff. She clutches it tightly.
Slowly, we close in on FRANCES. *And as we do so, we hear*
the whirling sound of the time release on the camera. It's the
same sound from earlier when REG *took the photo. The sound*
gets louder.
Louder.
Louder.
We see flashes of them on the cliff-top – happy, smiling. REG
and FRANCES *are happy and smiling . . .*
Then the shutter clicks.
Cut to black.

INT. RON'S FLAT, LIVING ROOM. DAY
RON, REG, PERRY *and* TERRY *are there. They are helping set*
up a glass tank for some snakes.
The phone rings . . .
RON *goes to answer phone.*

RON: . . . They relax me . . . I think they are beautiful.
    Don't you think? Lovely skin. (*Picks up phone.*) Hello
    . . . No, it's Ron . . . (*His expression changes.*)
    What. . . ? Yes . . . I see . . .
    REG *notices a change in* RON. RON *puts the phone down.*

REG *and* RON *stare at each other.*
REG (*flatly*): I know . . . Frances.

EXT. KRAY HOUSE. DAY
The whole of Vallance Road is full of flowers. Neighbours on either side of the street. A hearse, many cars.
   It's FRANCES' *funeral procession.*
   REG *comes out of the Kray house, supported by* VIOLET *and* RON. ROSE, MAY, IRIS, CHARLIE JUNIOR *follow. The immediate family get in the first cars and they pull away, following the hearse.*

INT. KRAY HOUSE, LIVING ROOM. DAY
It is after FRANCES' *funeral.*
   RON, REG, SAM RIPLEY, CHRIS RIPLEY, DEN *and* TIMMY. *Everyone is still dressed in black, very sombre, eating sandwiches and drinking.*
   REG *is just staring.*

RON: Did you hear that, Reg? The Pellams have been
      arrested. What about Cornell?
SAM: He's still on the loose. Shooting his mouth off.
CHRIS: And then there's Jack.
RON: Yes. There's always Jack. He's been calling me names.
      Very naughty.
   TIMMY *gets a plate of sandwiches and offers them to* REG.
TIMMY: Sandwich, Reg?
DENNIS: Leave it.
TIMMY: They're salmon.
DENNIS: Shut it.
   REG *continues staring.*

INT. EAST END PUB. DAY

A few scattered customers, BARMAID *wiping a table.* PERRY *and* STEVE *are enjoying a drink at the bar.*

PERRY: So Jack's done it again, eh?

STEVE: Two thousand quid this time.

PERRY: What is it with him?

STEVE: Fuck knows. Must have a death wish.

    Suddenly the door crashes open. JACK THE HAT *stumbles in. He's very, very, very drunk.*

STEVE: Jesus! Talk of the devil!

JACK: They treat me like a fucking kid. Well I was here when their mother was still wiping shit from their arses.

    STEVE *and* PERRY *rush up to quieten him.*

STEVE: Shut it, Jack! What's the bloody matter with you?

JACK (*shouts louder*): Their arses! You hear me!

PERRY: Quiet, Jack.

    JACK *pulls a gun from his pocket.*

JACK: You see that?

STEVE: Jeez, Jack!

PERRY: Put that down!

STEVE: Stop it now, Jack.

    A struggle ensues as STEVE *and* PERRY *try – as safely as possible – to get the gun from* JACK.

JACK (*screaming*): Ronnie! Reggie! I'm gonna get you! I'm going to get you!

BARMAID: Stop it! Stop it! Please!

JACK: Who're you telling what to do? You little slut!

    JACK *grabs a pint of beer. He throws it into* BARMAID*'s face. She screams.*

    STEVE *and* PERRY *snatch the gun from* JACK.

STEVE: That's it, Jack. Outside!

PERRY: Outside, Jack. Now.

    They drag him through the pub and –

JACK: I'LL KILL THE BASTARDS!!
   – *throw him outside.*

INT. KRAY HOUSE, BEDROOM. DAY
REG *is laying on top of the bed, fully dressed. He is staring blankly at the ceiling, very tearful.*

   VIOLET *is sitting on the edge of the mattress. She feels his forehead.*

VIOLET: You've got a temperature. Do you want anything
   to eat?
   REG *stares, sobs.*
VIOLET: Well, there's some biscuits on the saucer if you
   need something to pick at . . .
   REG*'s sobs increase.*
VIOLET: . . . Oh, Reg, please. You mustn't. We all lose
   people. Part of living is losing. But we have to move on.
   Reg? Reg . . . ?
REG: Oh, Mum –
   VIOLET *embraces him, crying with him.*
VIOLET: Oh, Reg. Don't, Reg. Mummy loves you. Mummy
   loves you.

EXT. GRAVEYARD. DAY
RON *and* VIOLET *amongst the tombstones, arm in arm.*

VIOLET: He's got to come to terms with it in his own way.
   Takes time. Time's a great healer.
RON: But you must speak to him, Mum.
VIOLET: I have spoken to him, for God's sake. What do you
   think I do? Sit up there and say nothing . . . (*Pause.*)
   You know I keep thinking about what your Aunt Rose
   said. About there being nothing under Victoria Park
   lake but bullets and babies . . . I've often thought about

111

it. Bullets and babies . . . Just think of it . . . All those
sad mothers . . . Sad mothers without children . . .
When you were a child they took you away from me.
Remember that? They said you were sick and they put
you in hospital. But it wasn't medicine you needed. It
was Reg.

VIOLET *holds* RON*'s hand. She stares at him intently.*

VIOLET: You've got to make him fight this. It's up to you
now, darling.

INT. KRAY HOUSE, BATHROOM. NIGHT

RON *is slooshing his face at the basin.*

He stares in the mirror.

His reflection stares back.

A very long, fateful beat –

INT. KRAY HOUSE, BEDROOM. NIGHT

REG *is curled on the bed, his eyes red with tears.*

RON *enters.*

He closes the door behind him and leans against it.

A long beat.

RON: It's crumbling, Reg. It's all falling apart. They're
laughing at us now. Jack the Hat's threatening us.
Walking round, proud as you like, waving a gun. Do
you hear me?

REG *doesn't respond.*

RON *goes to the bed, sits on the edge of the mattress.*
A beat.

RON: They're saying that we're through, Reg. That we're
over. *We're* over! Christ! Everything we've built!
Worked for! They're saying that there's nothing left.
That we're . . . burnt up. Falling!

REG *doesn't react.*

112

RON *stares at him.*

A beat.

RON: Well, do you know something? I think they're right.

REG *doesn't react.*

A beat.

RON: I said, I think they're right.

Still nothing.

A beat.

RON: I knew it was over. The moment Frances came along.

There's a flicker of reaction from REG.

RON *seizes his moment –*

RON: You forgot about me then, didn't you. About the
Firm. You were in love, so nothing else mattered. *I*
didn't matter. You just split us in two. So . . . you're
just going to leave me to do it all by myself, eh? Right! If
that's what you want, that's what I'll do. I'll get
Cornell. I'll get Jack the Hat. You just sit there. Don't
lift a fucking finger. Just sit there. And think about
Frances –

REG *reacts stronger, gets angry.*

Again, RON *seizes it –*

RON: Well it's over! She's dead! And it's over –

Suddenly REG *explodes.*

REG: You bastard!

REG *jumps on* RON, *grabs him round the throat.*

The two brothers struggle together.

RON: Hit me! Go on! Hit me! You think that's going to
answer it –

RON *pushes* REG *away.*

They stare at each other –

RON: Jesus Christ! There's a whole army of bastards out
there screaming for our blood. Why don't we help
them, eh? Let's kill each other.

REG *calms down.*

A beat.

> *Then, slowly,* REG *embraces* RON.

RON: I'm so sorry. I know how you must feel. Don't use it to hurt me, eh? Don't give them all that satisfaction. You know that . . . Like when we were kids, eh? Let's get them together.

> *A beat.*

REG: Let's get the bastards.

> *Now we reveal* REG's *hand.*
>> *He's been clutching something.*
>> *The silver crocodile brooch he'd given* FRANCES.
>> *The pin of the brooch has stabbed his palm.*
>> *His hand is full of blood.*
>> *Crocodile.*
>> *Red . . .*
>> *Silver . . .*

INT. REG'S CAR. NIGHT

The car is speeding along.
> *Lights flash by outside.*
> WHIP *is driving.*
> REG *is sitting in the back seat.*
> *He is neatly dressed in a black suit.*
> *His face is expressionless, eyes staring.*
> *He looks immaculate, lethal . . .*

INT. KRAY HOUSE, HALLWAY/LIVING ROOM. NIGHT

VIOLET *walks down the hallway with a cup of tea.*
> *The lighting in the house is subdued;* VIOLET *is settling in for an evening in front of the television.*
> *We see the television as* VIOLET *enters the living room.*
> *There's a black and white documentary about the Second World War on. In particular, the evacuation of children. We can hear the* TV NARRATOR.

TV NARRATOR:... and, as darkness consumed land after
   land, war became inevitable ...

INT. RON'S CAR. NIGHT
The car is speeding along.
   Lights flash by outside.
   PERRY *is driving.*
   RON *is sitting in the front seat.*
   He is neatly dressed in a black suit.
   His face is expressionless, eyes staring.
   He looks immaculate, lethal ...

INT. KRAY HOUSE, LIVING ROOM. NIGHT
VIOLET *sits on the sofa, intently watching television.*

TV NARRATOR:... they left their houses ...

INT. REG'S CAR. NIGHT
The car is still speeding.
   REG *is still staring ...*

INT. KRAY HOUSE, LIVING ROOM. NIGHT
VIOLET *watches television.*
   *She is involved in this programme now: reliving every
   moment of it.*

TV NARRATOR:... as they marched towards the destiny
   that fate had chosen for them. These boys...

INT. RON'S CAR. NIGHT
The car is still speeding.
RON *is still staring ...*

INT. PUB. NIGHT

JACK THE HAT *is sitting, drunkenly, at the bar.*
  Suddenly, STEVE *comes up.*
  He puts his arm round JACK's *shoulder.*

STEVE: Alright, Jack. Got a surprise . . .
  STEVE *pops a tablet into* JACK's *mouth.*
  JACK *smiles.*

EXT. SUZIE'S FLAT. NIGHT

A black car pulls up outside a basement flat.
  A party is in progress.
  STRAKER, TIMMY *and* DENNIS *get out of the car.*
  They're dressed very smart: on 'business'.
  They look at each other, then go down the steps to the
  basement.
  STRAKER *knocks on the door.*
  A blonde girl, SUZIE, *opens the door.*

STRAKER: Hello, Suzie.
  STRAKER, TIMMY *and* DENNIS *push their way into the*
  flat and –

INT. SUZIE'S FLAT, HALLWAY. NIGHT

  – SUZIE *stares with a mixture of tears and amazement.*
  STRAKER, TIMMY *and* DENNIS *push ruthlessly past her.*
  The party is in full swing.
  Lots of people, smoke, music . . .

STRAKER (*at* SUZIE): Having a nice party? Well you got to
  get everybody out.
TIMMY: Quick as you can.
DENNIS: There's a good girl.

117

STRAKER: We're having a meeting. (*Takes money from pocket and gives it to* SUZIE.) Here's twenty quid. Go find another party.

> SUZIE *hesitates, but only for a second, then . . .*

SUZIE: Okay, everyone! Listen! We've got to find another party!

> *The music stops . . .*

INT. PUB. NIGHT

JACK THE HAT *is dancing madly.*

> *The pills that* STEVE *has given him have obviously taken their effect.*
>
> STEVE *watches* JACK THE HAT, *claps, encourages him . . .*

INT. RON'S CAR. NIGHT

The car speeds along.

> RON *stares . . .*

INT. KRAY HOUSE, LIVING ROOM. NIGHT

VIOLET *watches TV . . .*

TV NARRATOR: . . . and childhood itself disappeared like the sands of time. . .

EXT. SUZIE'S FLAT. NIGHT

REG's *car pulls up.*

> REG *gets out.*
>
> *He goes down the stone steps and into the basement.*

INT. SUZIE'S FLAT, HALLWAY. NIGHT

REG *enters.*

The party guests have all gone now – only STRAKER,
TIMMY *and* DENNIS *are there.*
DENNIS *hands* REG *the gun.*

INT. SUZIE'S FLAT, LIVING ROOM. NIGHT
REG *enters.*
   He shakes hands with TIMMY *and* DENNIS.
   REG *sits in chair, holding gun and waiting . . .*

INT. PUB. NIGHT
STEVE *persuades* JACK THE HAT *to leave the pub.*

STEVE: Let's go to that party I was telling you about.

EXT. OUTSIDE BLIND BEGGAR PUB. NIGHT
RON'*s car pulls up.*
   RON *gets out of the car, holding the gun . . .*

INT. BLIND BEGGAR PUB. NIGHT
CORNELL *sits at the bar, drinking . . .*

EXT. BLIND BEGGAR PUB. NIGHT
RON *approaches the pub, clutching the gun . . .*
   He is excited, looking forward to it . . .

INT. BLIND BEGGAR PUB. NIGHT
RON *enters the pub.*
   He looks around, sees CORNELL.
   RON *casually approaches, aiming the gun at* CORNELL'*s
head.*
   CORNELL *sees the reflection of* RON *in the mirror.*

CORNELL: Well, well, well. Mr Kray.

CORNELL *turns to face* RON.

RON *aims the gun between* CORNELL's *eyes.*

CORNELL: You wouldn't dare.

RON *holds the gun firmly.*

RON *smiles.*

Then . . .

RON *pulls the trigger.*

The bullet hits CORNELL *between the eyes.*

Blood sprays over the mirror behind the bar . . .

EXT. OUTSIDE BLIND BEGGAR PUB. NIGHT

RON *comes out of the pub.*

He looks, if anything, exhilarated.

RON *gets into the car.*

The car drives off . . .

INT. KRAY HOUSE, LIVING ROOM. NIGHT

VIOLET *is beginning to weep at the television documentary now.*

All those children being separated from their mothers, tying on gasmasks etc.

TV NARRATOR: . . . for the children it was nothing more than an adventure. And instruments of survival were toys and playthings with which to amuse themselves . . .

EXT. PUB. NIGHT

STEVE *leads* JACK THE HAT *away from the pub.*

JACK THE HAT *needs a lot of help . . .*

INT. SUZIE'S FLAT. NIGHT

REG *is sitting in an armchair.*

He loads gun . . .

EXT. STREET. NIGHT
JACK THE HAT *and* STEVE *walk along . . .*

EXT. SUZIE'S FLAT. NIGHT
RON's *car pulls up.*
  RON *gets out of the car and approaches the flat . . .*

INT. KRAY HOUSE, LIVING ROOM. NIGHT
VIOLET *is beginning to sob now.*

TV NARRATOR: . . . the destruction was enormous. A kind
    of warfare never seen before. And only those who lived
    through it know what it took to survive . . .

INT. SUZIE'S FLAT. NIGHT
STRAKER *opens the door for* RON.
  RON *enters . . .*

INT. SUZIE'S FLAT. NIGHT
RON *walks in and looks at* REG.
  Then RON *turns off the light . . .*

EXT. SUZIE'S FLAT. NIGHT
JACK THE HAT *and* STEVE *approach the flat.*

STEVE (*laughing*): Go on. Get down there.
    JACK THE HAT *laughs.*
      STEVE *knocks on the door.*
      STRAKER *opens it.*
      JACK THE HAT *and* STEVE *enter . . .*

122

INT. SUZIE'S FLAT, LIVING ROOM. NIGHT

STEVE *pushes* JACK THE HAT *in.*

RON *flicks the light on.*

JACK THE HAT *sees* REG.

JACK *immediately sobers up.*

REG *aims the gun at* JACK.

JACK *begins to whimper.*

REG *presses the trigger.*

JACK *screams.*

Tighter on the trigger.

Then . . .

Click!

The gun will not fire.

REG (*panicking*): Ron! Ron!

JACK *goes to run.*

STEVE *and the others grab him.*

RON: You miserable old bastard.

REG: You've left us no choice, Jack.

JACK: No . . . Why . . . What have I done?

JACK *makes one last bid for freedom.*

He runs to a window.

Tries to get out.

Glass smashes.

But they drag him back.

JACK's *hat falls off.*

Suddenly, his is a bald, old man.

Even in the face of death, JACK *tries to conceal his baldness.*

He pathetically stretches his few remaining strands of hair over his scalp.

REG *hesitates, looks at* RON.

RON *gives* REG *a blade.*

RON: Kill him! Kill him!

The others are all in a frenzy of bloodlust now, urging REG
on.

ALL: Kill him! Kill him! Do it!

    REG *approaches* JACK *with the blade.*

JACK: You don't have to kill me.

ALL: Kill! Kill! Kill! Kill! Kill!

REG: Oh, yes I do.

    REG *plunges the blade into* JACK's *eye.*

       Blood spurts!

       JACK *falls to the floor.*

       REG *stabs him again.*

       Blood pumps from JACK's *mouth.*

       REG *keeps stabbing.*

       It is frantic.

       Blood!

       Stab!

       Blood!

       Stab!

       Blood! Blood! Blood!

       When JACK *finally stops struggling and is dead,* RON
       and REG *stand above him . . .*

INT. KRAY HOUSE, LIVING ROOM. NIGHT
VIOLET *is sobbing uncontrollably . . .*

INT. SUZIE'S FLAT, LIVING ROOM. NIGHT
The murder is now over.

   The TWINS *stare at each other.*

   Then they look in a mirror above the mantelpiece.

   *Their bloodstained reflections stare back at their bloodstained
selves.*

   *And their bloodstained reflections stare at their bloodstained
selves for a very, very, very long time . . .*

INT. KRAY HOUSE, LIVING ROOM. NIGHT

VIOLET *is still watching TV, although the programmes are*
long since over.
We get the impression it's the small hours of the morning.
The room is lit solely by the flashing, electric light of the TV
screen.
VIOLET *stares at it blankly.*
We hear the front door open and close, then REG *and* RON
come into the room.
VIOLET *does not react, it's as if she is in a trance.*

REG: You still up, Mum?

VIOLET: Just staring at the screen. It gets hypnotic after a
time.

RON: Well, you should turn it off . . . It's finished.
RON *turns the TV off.*
We see the flickering electric light disappear from
VIOLET*'s face.*
She looks at her boys.
A long beat.

VIOLET (*softly*): Shall I tell you my dream?

EXT. GRAVEYARD. DAY (1982)

It is VIOLET*'s funeral.*
Large crowds, journalists, cameras going off.
Both REG *and* RON *(much older now) are handcuffed to*
their respective guards.
They are standing by the graveside.
We see the tombstone with VIOLET*'s name.*
Flowers spelling the single word, 'MOTHER'.

VIOLET (*voice over*): I dreamt I was a beautiful white swan
. . . and . . . I could fly anywhere . . . do anything . . .
And I had this egg . . . a beautiful egg it was . . . And

there were noises coming from inside the shell . . . And
do you know what the noises were . . . They – now
listen carefully – they were children's voices . . . And I
looked after this egg. And I kept it safe and warm . . .
until one day . . . there was a hatching sound . . .

RON *and* REG *are staring at the grave.*

VIOLET (*voice over*): . . . and out came two perfect boys.
And they were mine. And they were wonderful . . .

EXT. SWAN IN FLIGHT. DAY
The black and white swan flies in slow motion again.
  Just like at the beginning of the film.
  But now . . .
  It's flying away from us.

VIOLET (*voice over*): . . . And they were perfect.

FADE TO BLACK.
ROLL CREDITS.

Methuen Modern Plays

include work by

Jean Anouilh
John Arden
Margaretta D'Arcy
Peter Barnes
Sebastian Barry
Brendan Behan
Edward Bond
Bertolt Brecht
Howard Brenton
Simon Burke
Jim Cartwright
Caryl Churchill
Noël Coward
Sarah Daniels
Nick Dear
Shelagh Delaney
David Edgar
Dario Fo
Michael Frayn
John Godber
Paul Godfrey
David Greig
John Guare
Peter Handke
Jonathan Harvey
Iain Heggie
Declan Hughes
Terry Johnson
Sarah Kane
Charlotte Keatley
Barrie Keeffe
Robert Lepage
Stephen Lowe

Doug Lucie
Martin McDonagh
John McGrath
David Mamet
Patrick Marber
Arthur Miller
Mtwa, Ngema & Simon
Tom Murphy
Phyllis Nagy
Peter Nichols
Joseph O'Connor
Joe Orton
Louise Page
Joe Penhall
Luigi Pirandello
Stephen Poliakoff
Franca Rame
Mark Ravenhill
Philip Ridley
Reginald Rose
David Rudkin
Willy Russell
Jean-Paul Sartre
Sam Shepard
Wole Soyinka
C. P. Taylor
Theatre de Complicite
Theatre Workshop
Sue Townsend
Judy Upton
Timberlake Wertenbaker
Victoria Wood

Methuen World Classics *and*
Methuen Contemporary Dramatists

Aeschylus (two volumes)
Jean Anouilh
John Arden (two volumes)
Arden & D'Arcy
Aristophanes (two volumes)
Aristophanes & Menander
Peter Barnes (three volumes)
Sebastian Barry
Brendan Behan
Aphra Behn
Edward Bond (five volumes)
Bertolt Brecht (six volumes)
Howard Brenton (two volumes)
Büchner
Bulgakov
Calderón
Jim Cartwright
Anton Chekhov
Caryl Churchill (two volumes)
Noël Coward (five volumes)
Sarah Daniels (two volumes)
Eduardo De Filippo
David Edgar (three volumes)
Euripides (three volumes)
Dario Fo (two volumes)
Michael Frayn (two volumes)
Max Frisch
Gorky
Harley Granville Barker
 (two volumes)
Peter Handke
Henrik Ibsen (six volumes)
Terry Johnson
Bernard-Marie Koltès

Lorca (three volumes)
David Mamet (three volumes)
Marivaux
Mustapha Matura
David Mercer (two volumes)
Arthur Miller (five volumes)
Anthony Minghella (two volumes)
Molière
Tom Murphy (four volumes)
Musset
Peter Nichols (two volumes)
Clifford Odets
Joe Orton
Philip Osment
Louise Page
A. W. Pinero
Luigi Pirandello
Stephen Poliakoff (two volumes)
Terence Rattigan
Christina Reid
Willy Russell
Ntozake Shange
Sam Shepard (two volumes)
Sophocles (two volumes)
Wole Soyinka
David Storey (two volumes)
August Strindberg (three volumes)
J. M. Synge
Sue Townsend
Ramón del Valle-Inclán
Frank Wedekind
Michael Wilcox
Oscar Wilde

Methuen Student Editions

For a Complete Catalogue of Methuen Drama titles
write to:

Methuen Drama
Random House
20 Vauxhall Bridge Road
London SW1V 2SA